RuleML for Policy Exchange

Project Report

by

Frank Appiah[1]

King's College London
School of Physical Sciences and Engineering

March 29, 2011

---

[1] All sentences or passages quoted in this report are my own work and other people's work that has been specifically acknowledged by clear cross-referencing to author and source.

Abstract

Engagement in e-commerce either B2B (Bussiness-to-Bussiness) or B2C (Bussiness-to-Consumer) require agents to be able to exchange and process policy rules so as to conform to policy formulations of the parties involved. In this report, I show an approach in capturing location-based and time-based access control policies with application to business policy rules within the existing syntax of RuleML. An E-Procurement sourcing case study is implemented as a working prototype system for these policies using the deductive reasoning engine, OO (Object-Oriented) jDREW and RDFS ontology. The case study uses a propositional language built from first-order logic and temporal logic to build a model for the prototype specification.

Keyword List :   Policies, Security, Trust, Location, Temporal Logic, Time.

Contents

List of Figures

Listings

List of Tables

Acronyms

B2B	–	Business-to-Business
B2C	–	Business-to-Comsumer
BU	–	Bottom Up
BO	–	Business Object
BOD	–	Business Object Document
DAML	–	DARPA Agent Markup Language
FOL	–	First Order Logic
jDREW	–	Java Deductive Reasoning Engine for the Web
KB	–	Knowledge Base
BPEL	–	Business Process Execution Language
UDDI	–	Universal Description Discovery and Integration
OWL	–	Web Ontology Language
RIF	–	Rule Interchange Format
Naf	–	Negation as failure
OOjDREW	–	Object Oriented java Deductive Reasoning Engine for the Web
OORuleML	–	Object-Oriented Rule Markup Language
POSL	–	Positional-Slotted Language
Prolog	–	PROgramming in LOGic
RDF	–	Resource Description Framework
RDFS	–	Resource Description Framework Schemas
SWRL	–	Semantic Web Rule Language
TD	–	Top Down
WRL	–	Web Rule Language
W3C	–	World Wide Web Consortium
XML	–	Extensible Markup Language

Chapter 1

Introduction

Electronic commerce, commonly known as (electronic marketing) e-commerce or eCommerce, consists of the buying and selling of products or services over electronic systems such as the internet and other computer networks(LAN[1], WAN[2], MAN[3] etc) within corporations. With the widespread use of the internet, the amount of trade conducted electronically in all spheres of our life has grown. A non-exhaustive list of applications of commerce in our world today are internet marketing, online transaction processing, electronic data interchange (EDI), automated order tracking, supply chain management, automated data collection systems, inventory management systems and billing systems.

E-commerce offers buyers maximum convenience. They can visit the web sites of multiple vendors round the clock a day to compare prices and make purchases, without having to leave their homes or offices from around the globe. In some cases, consumers can immediately obtain a product or service, such as an electronic book, a music file, or computer software, by downloading it over the Internet.

For sellers, e-commerce offers a way to cut costs and expand their markets. They do not need to build staff, or maintain a physical store or print and distribute mail order catalogs. Automated order tracking and billing systems cut additional labor costs, and if the product or service can be downloaded then e-commerce firms have no distribution costs involved.

Because the products can be sold over the global Internet, sellers have the potential to market their products or services globally and are not limited by the physical location of a store. Internet technologies also permit sellers to track the interests and preferences of their customers with the customer's permission and then use this information to build an ongoing relationship with the customer by customizing products and services to meet the customer's needs.

Relations among organisations involved in e-commerce are governed and guided by set of rules or policies. In simple terms, a policy describes a deliberate plan of action to guide decisions and achieve rational outcome. This numerous applications of e-commerce poses a lot of problems, one is making sure that rules or policies that are exchanged and processed by agents are interoperable with different stakeholders. The need for a common syntax for the exchange of policies or rules has become important in e-commerce. RuleML started in 2000 with XML-encoded positional-argument rules, and in 2002 they introduced frame-like knowledge representation (KR) with userlevel role-filler slots as unordered arguments. Since 2001 RuleML has permitted a kind of webizing to allow RDF-like [15] KR,

---

[1]LAN : Local Area Network
[2]WAN : Wide Area Network
[3]MAN : Metropolitan Area Network

and RuleML 0.91 has used URIs as optional additions to, or substitutes for, individual constants as well as relation and function symbols.

Main Contributions

This project presents a formal model for location-based and time-based access control policies built from a logical framework combining first-order logic, temporal logic and event calculus. The project also shows how the achieved theoretical structures in the LT access control policy can be represented in the syntax of RuleML in addition to the domain ontology of the access policy. Furthermore, an application of the logical framework to an E-Procurement subdomain involving a model of an E-Procurement domain ontology to describe concepts of the domain and reasoning about the domain information. Few policy rules collectively grouped under supplier refund policies, supplier discount policies and warranty policies are represented in the KB to provide a demonstrable evidence of application of the policies with the business processes generated.

The modelled information, access control policy rules, business policy rules in RuleML syntax and ontology definitions in RDFS are used in the deductive reasoning engine, OO jDREW to provide reasoning about information stored in the KB.

Organization

The rest of the report is organized in the following way. In C1.1 - C1.3 : discussion of the problem statement in relation to work previously done to serve as aims of the project, current state of the art and finally the formalization of a logical framework for the specification of the LT-Policy model. In C2, literature review of Rule Markup Language is discussed. I will look at the specification of the LT-Policy in C3 and overview of LT-RuleML syntax representation in C4 . C5 and C6 will provide an evaluation of the e-Procurement Knowledge base ,and concluding remarks respectively.

1.1 Discussions

This project focussed on location and time-based access control policies with business policies or rules in application to an E-Procurement subdomain. The project examines the acquisition of knowledge in the procurement subdomain and application of policies/rules on the KB. In Gao et al.[4] paper, they discussed how Geospatial-enabled RuleML can utilize spatial information in a semantic environment to enhance the ability to query and to represent health data. In their paper, a semantic health data query and representation framework was proposed through the formalization of spatial information. They included the geometric representation in RuleML deduction, and apply ontologies and rules for querying and representing health information. Corresponding geospatial built-ins were implemented as an extension to OO jDREW. The paper [4] also demonstrated the use of RuleML for geospatial-semantic querying and representing of health information via case studies in respiratory disease information. Rules and ontologies play an important role to automatically and contextually transform data, derive new conclusions and decisions from existing knowledge and act according to changed conditions and detected events (complex event processing). They identified few ontologies by following the disease taxonomy of respiratory diseases in the International Classification of Diseases (ICD-9).

Governatori et al. [6] presents an approach for the specification and implementation of e-contracts for Web monitoring and was done in the setting of RuleML. They argued that monitoring contract execution requires also a logical account of deontic concepts and of violations. They extended *RuleML* to cater for these claims. Their paper focused on transforming business contract rules from natural language into a machine readable, based on RuleML and executable form implemented as executable semantics. The logical framework used to analyse and represent the logical form is based on Deontic and Defeasible Logic.

The approach taken by Gao et al. and Governatori et al. has given me the impedus to this project but my work does not (solely) take into account of spatial representation of information and transformation of bussiness contract. Additionally, one can reason that location-based and temporal-based constrains are easily feasible to incorporate into business contract rules.

In summary, this project is concerned with satisfying these three objectives:

1. Developing a rich policy model for location-based and time-based access control policies.

2. Capturing the *location-based* and *time-based* access control policies within RuleML syntax.

3. Implementing an E-Procurement sourcing prototype of these policies with the deductive reasoning engine, OO jDREW.

1.2 State of the Art

RuleML[2] is a shared markup language that permits both forward(BU) and backward(TD) rules in XML for rewriting, deduction, and further inferential-transformational tasks. RuleML has evolved into DTDs-Schemas for positional-slotted RuleML sublanguages including Object-Oriented RuleML (OO RuleML).

The W3C aims to develop a standard for exchanging rules among disparate systems, especially on the Semantic Web called RIF[1]. The vision of RIF is a collection of dialects, an extensible set of languages with rigorously defined syntax and semantics.

BPEL[26] is an XML-based language which supports the web services technology stack, including SOAP, WSDL, UDDI, WS-Reliable Messaging, WS-Addressing, WS-Coordination and WS-Transaction. BPEL combines both WSFL (Web Services Flow Language) and XLANG approaches, and provides a rich vocabulary for description of business processes. The Business Process Execution Language enable the aggregation of existing web services into a more value-added web service. BPEL defines the composition by means of a workflow process consisting of a set of activities and the composition itself is exposed as a web service.

The adoption of a policy based-approach for controlling a system requires an appropriate policy representation and the design and development of a policy management framework [20]. It is important to highlight the existence of three languages for policy representation and reasoning including Ponder, Rei and KAoS. Ponder is a declarative, object oriented policy language for the management of distributed systems and networks. KAoS uses DAML and OWL as the basis for representing and reasoning about policies within Web Services, Grid Computing, and multi-agent system platforms [20]. Rei is a new deontic logic-based policy language that is grounded in a semantic representation of policies in RDF(S) and OWL-Lite.

An ontology is a formal representation of knowledge by a set of concepts within a domain and the relationships between these concepts. It is used to reason about the properties of that domain, and may be used to describe the domain. The need for an ontology language to encode the ontologies for reasoning about meanings has led to a numerous technologies including OWL[17](Web Ontology Language), RDF(S)[15] (Resource Definition Framework Schema), etc. Ontologies are now central to many applications such as scientific knowledge portals, information management and integration systems, electronic commerce, and semantic web services.

1.3 Preliminaries

In this section, I sketch the basics of the logical apparatus used in this project and a look at some basic definitions. The logical framework that will be used to reason in the policy formulation is based on the combination of First Order logic, Temporal Logic and Event Calculus. I will start with some basic notions: policy, right and permission related to security in the context of e-commerce and ontology.

Definition 1.3.1 (Policy) *A policy defines privacy requirements of a user, access permissions for a resource, rights of an individual to complete a transaction in an e-commerce setup (B2C or B2B).*

Security Policies concern issues of physical security, authentication, access control (AC), integrity, intrusion detection and audit trail. Authorisation policies are essentially security policies related to access-control and specify what activities a subject is permitted or forbidden to do, to a set of target resources. They are designed to protect target resources so are interpreted by access control agents or the run-time systems at the target system.

Definition 1.3.2 (Permission) *A permission is the named right to perform certain activities(action) on a target which is accompanied by constraints and requirements.*

Constraints express conditions that the end user must satisfy to be allowed to perform the corresponding activity, and requirements specify additional actions that the end user must execute.

Definition 1.3.3 (Right) *A right is a one-time(k-time) permission obtained in the context of e-commerce.*

Exercise of a consumable right can enable other rights for different subjects and objects. Access control policy can be seen as one policy amongst many that need to be managed and enforced in distributed system. The definition according to Maedche [23] is adopted here for this work to describe an ontology.

Definition 1.3.4 (Ontology) *An ontology structure $\mathcal{O}$ can be described by a 5-tuple consisting of the core elements of an ontology, i.e., concepts, relations, hierarchy, a function that relates concepts nontaxonomically and a set of axioms. The elements are defined as follows: $\mathcal{O} := \mathcal{C}, \mathcal{R}, \mathcal{H}^c, \mathcal{REL}, \mathcal{A}^o$ consisting of :*

- *Two disjoint sets, $\mathcal{C}$ (concepts) and $\mathcal{R}$ (relations)*

- *A **concept hierarchy**, $\mathcal{H}^c$: $\mathcal{H}^c$ is a directed relation $\mathcal{H}^d \subseteq \mathcal{C} \times \mathcal{C}$ which is called concept hierarchy or taxonomy. $\mathcal{H}^c$ ($\mathcal{C}_1, \mathcal{C}_2$) means $\mathcal{C}_1$ is a subconcept of $\mathcal{C}_2$*

- A *function* $\mathcal{REL} : \mathcal{R} \to \mathcal{C} \ X \ \mathcal{C}$ *that relates the concepts non taxonomically*

- *A set of ontology axioms* $\mathcal{A}^o$, *expressed in appropriate logical language.*

1.3.1 Logical Framework

In this section, I start by presenting the logical language which will be used throughout this report for the policy formalization. The propositional language been used here is derived from First-Order Logic [3], Temporal Logic [19] and Event Calculus [22]. In defining a generic model for a policy specification, First-Order Logic is used to define an interpretation relationships between all physical inputs from the set of notations, which are defined for an application-specific purpose. First-Order Logic provides both abstract and declarative model in describing specification relationships.

Let $\mathcal{L}$ be a propositional language defined over a set of atomic propositions: $\wedge$ stands for classical and, $\neg$ stands for classical negation, $\leftarrow$ stands for implication symbol and temporal operators; $\square$ (read as "**always**"); $\Diamond$ (read as "**eventually**"); $\bigcirc$ (read as "**next**"), $\mathcal{U}$ (read as "**until**") and $\mathcal{S}$ (read as "**since**").

From $\mathcal{L}$, we can distinguish the following four sets of formulas:

- The set $\mathcal{X}$ of rules.
- The set $\mathcal{SV}$ of state variables.
- The set $\mathcal{OC}$ of conditional objectives.
- The set $\mathcal{P}$ of policy rules.

Definition 1.3.5 *Let $\mathcal{F}$ be defined as the smallest set containing the propositional variables, $\forall P_v \in \mathcal{SV}$ that are closed under constructing new atomic formulas using the boolean connectives : $\neg$ and $\wedge$, and the temporal operators $\square$, $\Diamond$, $\bigcirc$, $\mathcal{U}$ and $\mathcal{S}$.*

A literal is either an atomic formula, $L(t_1, \ldots, t_n)$, (a positive literal) or the negation thereof, $\neg L(t_1, \ldots, t_n)$, (a negative literal) for which $L \in \mathcal{F}$.

Let's us now define the notion of rules, which is used to define structural facts in the knowledge base, $\mathcal{KB}$.

Definition 1.3.6 (Rules) *A rule, $\mathcal{R}$ is an expression of the form* $\forall x_1 \ldots \forall x_i \ (L(x_1, \ldots, x_i))$ *where* $\forall x_k \in \mathcal{SV}$.

For example, *sendMessage(sender, receiver, messageText)* is a rule and the state variables, $\mathcal{SV}$ are the sender, receiver and messageText. Let's now define the notion of *policy rules*, which is the building block for deriving goals from the knowledge base, $\mathcal{KB}$.

Definition 1.3.7 (Policy Rules) *A Policy Rule, $\mathcal{PR}$ is an expression of the form* $\forall x_1 \ldots \forall x_i \ (\mathcal{A}(x_1, \ldots, x_i)) \leftarrow \forall x_1 \ldots \forall x_i \ (L_1(x_1, \ldots, x_i) \wedge \ldots \wedge L_{n-1}(x_1, \ldots, x_i))$ *where* $\forall L_k \in \mathcal{OC}, \forall x_i \in \mathcal{SV}, \mathcal{A} \in \mathcal{X}$ *and* $\forall \mathcal{PR}_i \in \mathcal{P}$

A policy rule expresses that $\mathcal{A}$ is achieved if $L_1 \wedge \ldots \wedge L_{n-1}$ is achieved and the state variables, $x_1 \ldots x_i$ are used in the order expressed in $L_1 \wedge \ldots \wedge L_{n-1}$. The knowledge base, $\mathcal{KB}$ is equipped with three bases: a base $\mathcal{B}_r$ containing rules, a base $\mathcal{B}_p$ containing policy rules and a base $\mathcal{B}_o$ containing ontology definitions.

Definition 1.3.8 (Policy Base) *A Policy Base is equipped with three bases* $\langle \mathcal{B}_r, \mathcal{B}_p, \mathcal{B}_o \rangle$:

- $\mathcal{B}_r = \{(\mathcal{R}, b_i): \mathcal{R} \in \mathcal{KB}, b_i \in [0,1], i=1\ldots n\}$. *Pair* $(\mathcal{R}, b_i)$ *means that the rule* $\mathcal{R}$ *is certain to some degree* b_i.

- $\mathcal{B}_p = \{\mathcal{PR}_i: \mathcal{PR}_i \in \mathcal{P}, i=1\ldots m\}$. *Potential head*$(\mathcal{A}) = \{\exists L_1 \wedge \ldots \wedge L_n: \forall L_m \in \mathcal{OC}\}$

- $\mathcal{B}_o = \{\mathcal{O}\}$. *See 4.2.1 for explanation.*

Applying temporal logic

Temporal logic is used to describe any system of rules and symbolism for representing, and reasoning about propositions qualified in terms of time. The specification of any system of rules and symbolism in temporal logic is usually divided into safety conditions, liveness conditions, and fairness conditions. The standard notation for stating that formula f holds at state s in the structure $\mathcal{L}$ is: $\mathcal{L}, s \models f$. The temporal operators to be used are listed below, and the bold word in the description of the operator is the word to be visualized when reading the formula.

1. $\Diamond$ f : This means that **eventually f** will be true.

2. $\Box$ f : This means that **always f** will be true.

3. $\bigcirc$ f : This means that at the **next** state **f** will be true.

4. $e\ \mathcal{U}\ f$: This means that e is true **until** the state (instant in time) when f occurs. The strong **until** implies that f will eventually occur. In addition, e must always be true in the present.

Elements of T are called time points; if a pair (p; q) belongs to $<$ we say that p is earlier than q. For a point p, the set $\{q \in T \,|p < q\}$ will be called the future of p; the past of p is defined in the same manner.

The basic idea underlying temporal logic is to address issues by making valuations time-dependent; more precisely, one associates a separate valuation with each point of a given flow of time. Formally, Let $\mathcal{T} = (T, <)$ be the flow of time; a valuation on $\mathcal{T}$ is a map π: $(T \rightarrow (\phi \rightarrow \{0,1\}))$; ϕ denotes the set of propositional variables. For instance, one will say that the formula p $\wedge \neg$q is true at a time point t precisely if $\pi(t)(p) = 1$ and $\pi(t)(q) = 0$.

Event Calculus Basics

Central to Event Calculus is the notion of action occurrences, or events, at certain points in time. These events determine time intervals during which certain fluents hold [22]. An event is the occurrence of an action at a certain point in time. The Language, $\mathcal{L}$ uses the following predicates defined[22]:

- *holdsAt(f, t)* : Fluent f is true at timepoint t .

- *happens(e, t_1, t_2)* : Event e occurs from timepoint t_1 to timepoint t_2.

- *initiates(e, f, t_1)* : If event e occurs from timepoint t_1 to timepoint t_2, then fluent f will be true after t_2.

- *terminates(e, f, t_1)* : If event e occurs from timepoint t_1 to timepoint t_2, then fluent f will be false after t_2.

The occurrence of an event E at time T is denoted by *happens(E, T)*. An event can initiate or terminate fluents, depending on the action associated with the event, *initiates(E,P)* (*terminates(E, P)*) means that event E initiates (terminates) the fluent P. The atom *act(E, A)* denotes that E consists of an occurrence of action A.

The frame axiom in Event Calculus:

holds(P, T) ← happens(E_1, T_1), T_1 < T, initiates(E_1, P), ¬clipped(T_1, P, T).

clipped(T_1, P, T) ← happens(E_2, T_2), T_1<T_2, T_2<T, terminates(E_2, P).

In all cases, any FOL axioms can be added to the theory. At the beginning of time, say at t_0, there is a start event initiating all fluents that are initially true. This is represented by including the following clauses in the definition of the predicates time, happens and initiates:

time(t_0).

happens(start, t_0).

initiates(start, P) ← initially(P).

Chapter 2

Literature Review

2.1 Contributions and Importance of RuleML

This section provides an introductory material to RuleML, current contributions made to the development of RuleML and importance(uses) of RuleML in the current state of the policy exchange languages.

2.1.1 Introduction to RuleML

The main mission statement of the Rule Markup Initiative is to develop RuleML as the canonical Web language for rules using XML markup, formal semantics, and efficient implementations [2]. In the sense of efficient implementation, this project will use Object-Oriented jDREW for the implementation of the modelled policies as an extension to OO jDREW. The Rule Markup Initiative has taken steps towards defining a shared Rule Markup Language, permitting both forward (BU) and backward (TD) rules in XML for deduction, rewriting, and further inferential-transformational tasks. RuleML provides a way of expressing business rules in modular stand-alone units. It enables the deployment, execution, and exchange of rules between different systems (platform independent because it is using XML markup) and tools.

2.1.2 Contributions of RuleML

Premises and Conclusions. Premises or conclusions are induced from the representation of predicates (atoms) in *RuleML*. A predicate is an n-ary relation and it is defined as an <Atom> element in *RuleML* with the following DTD definition.

```
<!ELEMENT Atom (Rel, (Ind | Var)*)>
<!ELEMENT Rel (#PCDATA)>
<!ELEMENT Var (#PCDATA)>
<!ELEMENT Ind (#PCDATA)>
```

Example 2.1.1 *<Atom>*
<Rel>sendPurchaseMail</Rel>
<Ind>Good</Ind>
<Ind>PurchaseOrderDate</Ind>
<Ind>DeliveryDate</Ind>
</Atom>

Derivation Rules. Derivation Rules are special reaction rules whose action is to add a conclusion when certain conditions have been met. They comprise one or more conditions but derive only one conclusion. These rules can be applied in a forward or backward manner, the latter reducing the proof of a goal (conclusion) to proofs of all its subgoals (conditions)[12]. Derivation Rules allow the derivation of information from existing rules [13]. For example, a customer is labelled as a "Premium" customer when he buys $88 worth of coffee in a cafe restaurant. As such, the rule here states that the customer must spent on coffee, thus deriving the information here that the customer is a "Premium" customer. Derivation rules have the following syntax:

```
<!ELEMENT Implies (( head, body ) | ( body | head ))>
<!ELEMENT body (And)>
<!ELEMENT head (Atom)>
<!ELEMENT And (Atom+)>
```

Example 2.1.2 (Rule) *A customer is premium if their location is in "193.122.33.99" and their spending has been min 5000 euro in the previous year.*

In RuleML :

```
<Implies>
  <head>
    <Atom>
      <opr>
      <rel>premium</rel>
      </opr>
      <var>customer</var>
    </Atom>
  </head>
  <body>
    <And>
      <Atom>
        <opr>
        <rel>location</rel>
        </opr>
        <var>193.122.33.99</var>
      </Atom>
      <Atom>
        <opr>
        <rel>spending</rel>
        </opr>
        <var>customer</var>
        <ind>min 5000 euro</ind>
        <ind>previous year</ind>
      </Atom>
    </And>
  </body>
</Implies>
```

Facts. Facts are considered as special derivation rules but without the specification of conjunction of premises or conditions **body** [12]. They denote simple pieces of information that are deemed to be true. URLs/URIs can also be embedded within facts to reference the elements that are being referred to. Facts have the following syntax:

```
<!ELEMENT Fact (Atom)>
```

A fact element uses just a conclusion role "head", meaning whatever is included in the "head" is understood as true [13].

Example 2.1.3 (Fact 1) *Consider a ternary offer relation applied to ordered arguments for the offer name, category, and price. In the PR syntax an offer of an "mobile" can be categorized as "vodaphone" and priced at \$230 via the following fact (Prolog-like, except that a capitalized symbol like Mobile denotes an individual constant, not a variable):*

```
offer(Mobile, vodaphone, 230).
```

In RuleML:

```
<Fact>
  <Atom>
   <Rel>offer</Rel>
    <Ind>Mobile</Ind>
    <Ind>vodaphone</Ind>
    <Ind>230</Ind>
  </Atom>
</Fact>
```

Queries. As in many deduction approaches, RuleML queries are regarded as headless implications, symmetrically to regarding facts as bodiless implications. They enumerate the bindings of all their free (existentially interpreted) variables. This query incorporation into RuleML assumes that the sublanguage expressiveness should be the same for "assertions" (facts and imps) and for the "requests" (queries) on them.

2.1.3 Importance of RuleML

Rules are being used for many interconnected purposes, capturing regularities in application domains such as the following [2]:

Engineering: Diagnosis rules that appreciates model-based approaches and combines with rules, as described by Adnan Darwiche in Model-based diagnosis under real-world constraints, AI Magazine, Summer 2000.

Commerce: Business rules including XML versions such as the Business Rules Markup Language (BRML).

Internet: Access authentication as proposed by Tim Berners-Lee for the authentication rules.

Law: Legal reasoning has been formalized by Robert Kowalski and Marek Sergot in an Imperial College Group.

Chapter 3

LT-Policy

The specification of LT-Policy is a policy formulated from the specification of other policy models in [28], [27], [36], [37] and this did serve as an advantage in the formal reasoning. The policy is comprised of location and time policies with time usage control constrains, which is much of a common use in e-commerce setups. The fundamental idea is that an access to a resource, provision of a service or process request evaluation of a subject in any domain of commerce take into account the *location of subject* and *time of request* with the persistent knowledge base. For example, when the nightly batch-processing agent authenticates, or logs into the system, a subject that represents the agent is created, and the appropriate permissions are associated with that subject. Authorization has to play a crucial role in maintaining and strengthening a location policy.

Each policy rule in LT-Policy Program is of the form:

$A \leftarrow L_1 \wedge \ldots \wedge L_{n-1}$, where n $\geq$ 1.

Here and in the rest of this report, as notation for LT-policy, I am employing an extended form of the Prolog-like notation for declarative policy that is typically used in policy literatures [29] with additional temporal operators. The outcome of the rules derived from this specification of LT-policy is represented in the syntax of RuleML, which is LT-RuleML in C4 . By "rule" in this report, I mean more specifically an implication (i.e., IF-THEN) in which the IF part may contain multiple conjunction (i.e., ANDed conditions.)

3.1 Location and Time Context Model

In the context of access control, the notion of an authorization is of central importance. Declarative policies guide the behavior of entities in open, distributed environments via:

1. Positive and negative authorizations ,and obligations.

2. Focus on domain actions, including communicative acts for agent communication.

3. Policies that are based on attributes of the action and its actor and target.

The focus here is on both positive and negative authorization ,and authentication. The assumption made for this model is that the subject is post-authenticated. Lets begin by defining the sets of notations that are used in the formulation of authorization :

- A set $\mathcal{S}$ of subject identifiers: s_1, s_2, ..., s_n;

- A set $\mathcal{R}$ of resources: $r_1, r_2, \ldots, r_n$;

- A set $\mathcal{A}$ of access privileges: $a_1, a_2, \ldots, a_n$;

- A set $\mathcal{L}$ of locations: $l_1, l_2, \ldots, l_n$;

- A set $\mathcal{T}$ of time points: $t_1, t_2, \ldots, t_n$;

- A set $\mathcal{C}$ of credentials: $c_1, c_2, \ldots, c_n$.

In the LT-Policy Model, A logical location $l \in \mathcal{L}$ is an abstract notion that characterises many physical locations with application-specific attributes, like *City, Baggage Claim Area, Entertainment Venues, Patients Home, Airport, IP Address.* Time is seen as a sequence of discrete time points t in the flow of time. An interval $\mathcal{INT}$ is a set of time instances, for example from 11am to 7pm on every weekdays. Locations are assigned to subjects at any time point. Permissions are assigned to resources during a time interval and according to the subject's location. A subject s may be permitted or disallowed an access privilege a on a resource r if and only if s can activate an action to which the access privilege a on r is also assigned. To activate an action, the subject must be in a location and during a time interval where the activation can take place.

> The set of authorizations $\mathcal{AUTHZ}$ is composed by tuples $\langle s, a, r, l, t \rangle$ that expresses the fact that the subject s has the access a privilege on the resource r at time t and situated at location or site l.

The following interpretation relationships are generated for the authorization model:

- $\forall s \in \mathcal{S}, \forall a \in \mathcal{A}, \forall r \in \mathcal{R}, \forall l \in \mathcal{L}, \exists t \in \mathcal{T}$: authorized($s, a, r, l, t$)

- $\forall s \in \mathcal{S}, \forall a \in \mathcal{A}, \forall r \in \mathcal{R}, \forall l \in \mathcal{L}, \exists t \in \mathcal{T}$: permission($s, a, r, l, t$)

- $\forall s \in \mathcal{S}, \forall a \in \mathcal{A}, \forall r \in \mathcal{R}, \forall l \in \mathcal{L}, \exists t \in \mathcal{T}$: prohibition($s, a, r, l, t$)

$\square$ V(s, a, r, l, t) $\in \mathcal{AUTHZ} \iff \mathcal{U}$ (($\forall s \in \mathcal{S}$) $\land$ ($\forall a \in \mathcal{A}$) $\land$ ($\forall r \in \mathcal{R}$) $\land$ ($\forall l \in \mathcal{L}$) $\land$ ($\forall t \in \mathcal{T}$)) where V $\in$ relationSet={authorized, permission, prohibition}.

> **Discussion:** The above can be described as that the relation V(s, a, r, l, t) is **always** in $\mathcal{AUTHZ}$ **until** for all state variables s is in $\mathcal{S}$, a is in $\mathcal{A}$, r is in $\mathcal{R}$, l is in $\mathcal{L}$ and there exist t in $\mathcal{T}$.

For example, A manager may be permitted to read the employee document within the week days from 7AM to 6PM if the manager is in the company office. This can be interpreted with the *permission* relationship as:

```
permission(manager, read, employee_doc, company_office, [WEEK+7AM,WEEK+6PM]).
```

A positive authorization, $+(s, a, r, l, t)$ denotes that subject s has a access on resource r at a specific time points, t $[t_1, t_2]$ and location, l. A negative authorization, $-(s, a, r, l, t)$ denotes that subject s is denied a access on r resource at a specific time points, t $[t_1, t_2]$ and location, l. Refrain policies specify what a subject must refrain from doing and are similar to negative authorization policies but are interpreted by the subject. Negative authorization is for expressing exceptions and open policies.

3.1.1 Evaluating access request

A subject $s \in \mathcal{S}$ is permitted to perform an action $a \in \mathcal{A}$ on an resource $r \in \mathcal{R}$ if and only if s at time $t \in \mathcal{T}$, being in location $l \in \mathcal{L}$, can activate action $a \in \mathcal{A}$ to which an access on r has been assigned at time t and location l.

Example 3.1.1 *Suppose that two subjects s_1 and s_2 are permitted actions a_1 and a_2 on resources r_1 and r_2 which are situated in locations l_1 and l_2. If the subjects s_1 and s_2 are bounded by specific time points t_1 and t_2 that elapses to make the action disabled. This access request is then represented using the authorized relation as:*

- *authorized(s_1, a_1, r_1, l_1, t_1)*

- *authorized(s_2, a_2, r_2, l_2, t_2)*

Discussion: By inspection, it can be deduce from the example that the set of authorizations that are included in $\mathcal{AUTHZ}$ is:
{ authorized(s_1, a_1, r_1, l_1, t_1), authorized(s_2, a_2, r_2, l_2, t_2) }.

Example 3.1.2 (Applying temporal operator, $\square$) *The temporal operator, $\square$ is applied to Example 3.1.1 to provide a means of describing global requirements or axioms for an authorization. This access request is then represented using the temporal authorized relation:*

- *$\square$ authorized(s_1, a_1, r_1, l_1, t_1)*

- *$\square$ authorized(s_2, a_2, r_2, l_2, t_2)*

Discussion: From Example 3.1.2 , it is **always** the case that the subject, s is authorized to perform action, a on resource, r that is located at site, l within the specific time point, t.

3.1.2 Action and ActionHistory: Action Trace

Events provide a homogeneous basis for representing change, a feature that is an essential aspect of agents (business partners, process, procedural call) in distributed systems (e-commerce setup). In e-commerce, a subject's action status is determined from the actions that are recorded as part of the event descriptions that relate to a *Subject s*. Events can be viewed as a structure, described via a sequence of ground terms of the form:
actionHistory(e_i, s, a, r, t) where *actionHistory* is a data constructor of arity five, e_i denotes a unique event identifier, s identifies a subject, a is an action on resource r associated to the event, and t is the *time* at which the event happened. The semantics of [27] is defined over traces with discrete time steps. At each time step, a set of events can occur. An event corresponds to the execution of an action. Each event belongs to an event class. Possible event classes include usage and other, the latter standing for all non-usage events, e.g., purchase orders, invoices recepient, payments or notifications.
The following types of relation for action are generated:

- action enabling: *enact(a, l, t)* if action a enabled at time t and location l.

- action disabling: *disenact(a, l, t)* if action *a* disabled at time *t* and location *l*. The semantics of *disenact(a_1, l, t)* is also represented when there is no explicit declaration of *enact(a_1, l, t)*.

- action trace: *actionHistory(e_i, s, a, r, t)*.
  actionHistory(e_i, s, a, r, t) ← act(e_i, a) ∧ happens(e_i, t) ∧ attribute(s, r).
  The history of an action is actually recorded if there is an association of an event with the action and the event happened within the specific time point, *t* ,and the two attributes (subject and resource) are defined accordingly.

Example 3.1.3 *The access requests in Example 3.1.1 are possible to execute actions a_1 and a_2 at specified locations, l_1 and l_2 within the specified time points t_1 and t_2 if the following are defined:*

- $\forall (a_1, l_1, t_1) \in \mathcal{ALT}$: *enact($a_1$, l_1, t_1)*.

- $\forall (a_1, l_1, t_1) \in \mathcal{ALT}$: *enact($a_2$, l_2, t_2)*.

Discussion: The action a_i is enabled at the locations l_i only for the specified time points t_i if all the state variables are declared in the set of access privileges $\mathcal{A}$, locations $\mathcal{L}$ and time points $\mathcal{T}$ respectively where i>0.

Example 3.1.4 (Applying temporal operator, □) *The temporal operator, □(read as "always") is applied to Example 3.1.3 to generate an ordered relation:*

- $\forall (a_1, l_1, t_1) \in \mathcal{ALT}$: □ *enact($a_1$, l_1, t_1)*.

- $\forall (a_1, l_1, t_1) \in \mathcal{ALT}$: □ *enact($a_2$, l_2, t_2)*.

Discussion: The action a_i is **always** enabled at the locations l_i only for the specified time points t_i if all the state variables are declared in the set of access priveleges $\mathcal{A}$, locations $\mathcal{L}$ and time points $\mathcal{T}$ respectively where i>0.

3.1.3 Authorization Policy Rule

The authorization components made up with *permission, prohibition, authorized, disenact* and *enact* interpretation relationships can be combined using first-order logical operators to describe more complex requirements. There are four possible authorization options for illustrating an authorization concept but only these two are used in this work to provide an authorization:

- authorized(s, a, r, l, t) ← permission(s, a, r, l, t) ∧ enact(a, l, t).

- ¬authorized(s, a, r, l, t) ← prohibition(s, a, r, l, t) ∧ disenact(a, l, t).

Example 3.1.5 *The examples in Example 3.1.1 and Example 3.1.3 are combined to form a complex policy rule using the authorization policy rule explained above. These policies are generated :*

- $\forall (s_1, a_1, r_1, l_1, t_1) \in \mathcal{SARLT}$: *authorized($s_1$, a_1, r_1, l_1, t_1) ← permission(s_1, a_1, r_1, l_1, t_1) ∧ enact(a_1, l_1, t_1)*.

- $\forall(s_2, a_2, r_2, l_2, t_2) \in \mathcal{SARLT}$: *authorized*($s_2, a_2, r_2, l_2, t_2$) ← *permission*($s_2, a_2, r_2, l_2, t_2$) ∧ *enact*($a_2, l_2, t_2$).

Discussion: For each subject, s_i performing an action, a_i on resource, r_i situated at location, l_i within the time point, t_i will be authorised to do so if there is a permission declared in $\mathcal{KB}$ for that subject s_i with a specific action, a_i on resource, r_i situated at location, l_i within the time point, t_i and the action, a_i is enabled at location, l_i within the time points, t_i. For this to be possible the variables s, a, r, l and t should be from the set of formulas $\mathcal{S}$, $\mathcal{A}$, $\mathcal{R}$, $\mathcal{L}$ and $\mathcal{T}$ respectively.

Example 3.1.6 (Applying temporal operators: □, ◊) *The temporal operators □ and ◊ are applied to the Example 3.1.5 to generate a complex relationships below:*

- $\forall(s_1, a_1, r_1, l_1, t_1) \in \mathcal{SARLT}$: ◊ *authorized*($s_1, a_1, r_1, l_1, t_1$) ← □ *permission*($s_1, a_1, r_1, l_1, t_1$) ∧ □ *enact*($a_1, l_1, t_1$).

- $\forall(s_2, a_2, r_2, l_2, t_2) \in \mathcal{SARLT}$: ◊ *authorized*($s_2, a_2, r_2, l_2, t_2$) ← □ *permission*($s_2, a_2, r_2, l_2, t_2$) ∧ □ *enact*($a_2, l_2, t_2$).

Discussion: From the Example 3.1.6, you can deduce that for each subject, s performing an action, a on resource, r situated at location, l within the time points, t will **eventually** be authorised to do so if there is **always** a permission declared for that subject s with a specific action, a on resource, r situated at location, l within the time points, t and the action, a is **always** enabled at location, l within the time points, t. For this to be possible the variables s, a, r, l and t should be from the set of formulas $\mathcal{S}$, $\mathcal{A}$, $\mathcal{R}$, $\mathcal{L}$ and $\mathcal{T}$ respectively.

3.1.4 Domain Knowledge

From the achieved access control policy, the following domain knowledge is acquired to represent this policy in the RuleML syntax:

- Actor: The subject whom a permission or prohibition has been assigned to is defined as an actor in the ontology definition. For example, an actor can be a client, payee, manufacturer, organisation, payer etc.

- Action: The action permitted or prohibited by a subject is represented as an Action ontology definition. For example, an action can be desptach, payment, issue of quote, issue of invoice etc.

- Entity: An entity is the resource on which the action is performed on. This can be a delivery note, quotation, invoice, request purchase order.

- Place: This defined ontology is used to represent location in the access control.

Chapter 4

LT-Policy in RuleML: Syntax Representation

In this C4 , I will illustrate how to use LT-policy to represent e-commerce rules with a long concise case study in E-Procurement sourcing. As we go, I will describe some more of the LT KR's technical aspects and advantages. RuleML is, at its heart, an XML[21] syntax for rule knowledge representation (KR), that is interoperable among major commercial rule systems[29]. Business rules are the controls an organization puts in place to ensure the:

- consistent behavior of its business processes across all channels.

- validity of its knowledge base.

Business rules are expressed using the vocabulary of the business. Business rules need to be directly associated with the business processes they control. Business rules are supported by the organization's information technology. Business rules need to be expressed in a grammar that structures rule statements in a manner that allow them to be analyzed and reporting on as a set, whether or not they are enforced through information technology. Policies provide high-level control of entities in the environment. Using policies reduces the need to modify code in order to change systems' behavior.

4.1 Case Study

In this section, I will discuss a case study in the eProcurement subdomain (i.e., (B2B) purchasing and selling goods and services over the Internet) based on a storyboard used in [24]. Procurement is an integral part of B2B processes and an essential part of any organisations ability to function effectively but has only recently emerged as an important topic within the fast growing B2B e-commerce market. The case study presented in this report examines the analysis of the purchasing process and the definition of the functional specifications of an e-procurement sourcing system.

> ACME manufacturer (client) sends a request for quotation (RFQ) to the EMCA provider (supplier). The supplier processes the RFQ and sends back his quotation to the client. The client evaluates the quotation and, possibly, makes the purchase order (PO) that is sent to the supplier. The supplier accepts the purchase order, fulfills it, delivers the goods, and sends the

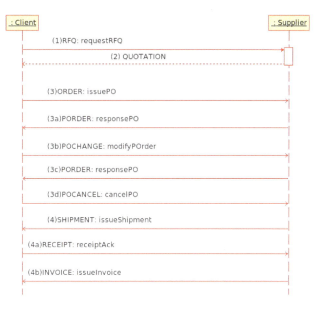

Figure 4.1: Client-Supplier Interaction

invoice to the client. Finally, if the delivered goods correspond to the order, the client pays the invoice.

For example, rules are useful in describing [29] :

- service provisions, e.g., rules for refunds;

- surrounding business processes, e.g., rules for lead time to place an order, rules about cancelling orders.

- terms and conditions, e.g., rules for price discounting;

- Policies about discounting for groups or preferred customer organizations, e.g., hotel discounts for premium members, are often similar in feel to the example above about personalized discounting.

- Policies about creditworthiness, trustworthiness, and authorization are often naturally expressed in terms of sufficient and/or necessary conditions. Such conditions include: credentials, e.g., credit ratings or professional certifications; third-party recommendations; properties of a transaction in question, e.g., its size or mode of payment; and historical experience between the agents, e.g., familiarity or satisfaction.

Example 4.1.1 (Supplier Refund Policy) *A typical example of a supplier's refund policy are:*

- *(Rule A:) If client returns the purchased good for any reason, within 25 days, then the purchase amount, minus a 14 percent restocking fee, will be refunded.*

- *(Rule B:) If client returns the purchased good because it is defective, within 1 year, then the full purchase amount will be refunded.*

Suppliers often provide personalized price discounting. A topic of considerable interest today among e-commerce suppliers is how to do this more cheaply and uniformly by automating it.

Example 4.1.2 (Supplier Discount Policy) *A typical example of a supplier's discount policy are:*

- *(Rule A:) 5 percent discount if client has a history of loyal spending with the supplier.*

- *(Rule B:) 10 percent discount if client has a history of big spending with the supplier.*

- *(Rule C:) 5 percent discount if client has a provider charge card.*

- *(Rule D:) 10 percent discount if client is a member of the supplier's Platinum Club.*

- *(Rule E:) No discount if client has a late-payment history during the last year.*

Example 4.1.3 (Warranty (Category) Policy) *The warranty of a good can be based on category or not :*

- *(Rule A:) 2 years warranty if the good is part of a particular good category.*

- *(Rule B:) 1 year warranty for all goods.*

4.2 Knowledge Base Design: Ontology, Facts and Rules

In this section, I give a brief introduction to ontologies and how light-weight RDFS ontologies are used to structure the facts in the eProcurement KB. Ontologies represent the real world in a systematically structured way. RDFS provides modeling primitives for organizing (Web) objects into hierarchies. It is viewed as a basic language for writing light-weight ontologies that are *subClassOf* taxonomy. In RDFS, objects sharing similar characteristics can be typed with classes. The concepts (or classes) of the e-Procurement subdomains in RDF Schema (RDFS) light-weight ontologies are adapted from the defined ontologies in [24]. Classes can be grouped into hierarchies through the *subClassOf* relationship: a class S is a subclass of a class T if every instance of S is also an instance of T. Examples of eProcurement classes are actors, entities: business object documents, attributes of entities, actions, etc. All classes in the e-Procurement ontology is a subclass of the Thing class. These, three basic categories were identified in [24] for modeling the concepts in the e-Procurement subdomain:

1. Business Actor (BA)

2. Business Process (BP)

3. Business Object (BO)

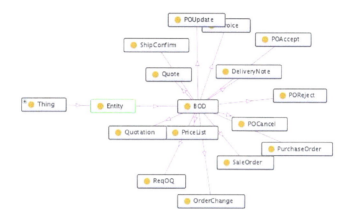

Figure 4.2: Entity Ontology Class

4.2.1 Knowledge Design: eProcurement Ontology

Entity

Business process operates on an entity. Here Entity is the superclass of business object document and a business object document (BOD) is a further refinement of a BO that represents a category of documents in the business domain. The entity class has a subclass, BOD and BOD is further subclassified into smaller classes. This diagram was produced by Protege. An excerpt from the RDFS taxonomy describing a portion of the *subClassOf* hierarchy for the entity class is shown in Figure 4.2.

Actor

The active elements of a business domain, able to activate, perform, or monitor a business process. Domain Experts, in analyzing the reality, are asked to identify relevant actors that operate producing, updating or consuming business objects(BOs). The Actor class is further sub-classified into smaller classes as shown in Figure 4.3.

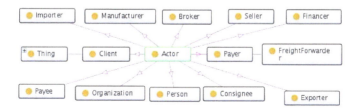

Figure 4.3: Actor Ontology Class

ActionStatus

The ActionStatus class has basically three subclasses namely: *Active* class, *InActive* class and *Suspended* class. The ActionStatus class is further subclassified into smaller classes as shown in Figure 4.4. An excerpt from the RDFS taxonomy describing a portion of the *subClassOf* hierarchy for the ActionStatus class is shown below.

Figure 4.4: ActionStatus Ontology Class

Action

A business activity or operation aimed at the satisfaction of a business goal, operating on a set of BOs (e.g.,purchase order issuing, requesting quotation). It can be rather simple, with a limited duration in time, or complex, with parallel branches and phases that last for a long time span. The Action class is further sub-classified into smaller classes as shown in Figure 4.5.

Figure 4.5: Action Ontology Class

Message

A message represents the information exchanged during an interaction (e.g.,request, response) between processes, more specifically on exchange information. A message is characterized by a content that is typically a BOD (e.g.,a RFQ-message, carrying a request for quotation). FIPA approach is adopted here which is based on 23 message types related to different kinds of communicative acts. Specifically, 8 message kinds are selected, which the payload matches a BOD in the eProcurement ontology in [24]. The Message class is further sub-classified into smaller classes as shown in Figure 4.6.

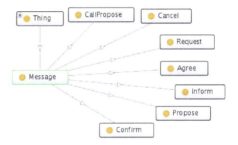

Figure 4.6: Message Ontology Class

Attribute

Attributes characterize the information structure of a concept. In OPAL there are atomic attributes, modeling elementary information (e.g.,streetname), and complex attributes, modeling structured information (e.g.,address). Essentially, a complex attribute is defined as an aggregation of lower level complex and/or atomic attributes. An excerpt from the RDFS taxonomy describing a portion of the *subClassOf* hierarchy for the Attribute class is shown in Figure 4.7.

4.2.2 Partonomy of Business Processes

Partonomy is a classification based on part-of relation. The workflow of a business process is represented as a *partOfProcess* relation generated to define facts in the knowledge base. A logical variable called *?relatedTo* is added to any business process relation to convey the sub-process. An excerpt workflow of the ordering business process is shown below :

partOfProcess(order, issuePO).
partOfProcess(order, responsePO).
partOfProcess(order, requestPOChange).
partOfProcess(order, changePO).
partOfProcess(order, cancelPO).

The partonomy specification relationship, **partOfProcess** describes that *issuePO, responsePO, requestPOChange, changePO* and *cancelPO* processes are **always** part of the *order* process. The complete partonomy specification of the business processes can be referred from Appendix C, Listing 4 and the RuleML syntax representation in Appendix C, Listing 5:Lines 35-112.

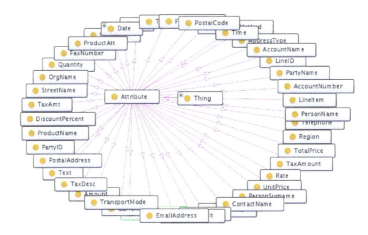

Figure 4.7: Attribute Ontology Class

4.2.3 Knowledge Design: Facts

The partonomy of the business processes in Section 4.2.2 depicts the functional capabilities in the e-Procurement business domain. In order to reason about the knowledge base, there need to be structural facts for this to be successful and the information for the KB is based on both Common Procurement Vocabulary[1] and self-constructed information for evaluation purposes. The facts will be represented in RuleML using RuleML slots feature and the e-Procurement ontology classes for the type definition of the domain. In this section, the focus is on the sourcing business process and this is thoroughly discussed ,and the technical KR aspects are look into.

Sourcing Business Process

The sourcing business process is comprised of these sub-processes: requesting of a quote, distributing of price lists and the issuing of quote. The sourcing process depends on other factor like quantity, cost ,time and place of the purchase order. In order to distribute the price lists of goods, there need to be a list of products with its associated unit price in the knowledge base. The *product* relation is generated to cater for the goods knowledge base. For example, a product in the KB is defined as:

```
product(?id, ?name, ?code, ?price, ?att, ?quantity, ?manufacturer,
?supplier, ?description, ?category).
```

The names after the : symbol is a class in the e-Procurement ontology defined in Appendix D, Listing 6 whiles the ? symbol depicts the logical variables which is to be replaced by real values in the KB. The class **ProductAtt** is used to define any attribute class of the product if not explicitly defined in the ontology. The following process relations are defined:

---

[1]Common Procurement Vocabulary. http://www.cpvclassification.com/

- *requestQuote(?id, ?bod, ?actor, ?location, ?requestDate, ?relatedTo).*

- *issueQuote(?bod:Quote, ?relatedTo).*

- *sendPriceList(?bod, ?code, ?name, ?price, ?man, ?processDate, ?relatedTo).*

- *supplier(?name, ?description, ?transport, ?telephone, ?city, ?webpage, ?role).*

Product Category

The primary list of product categories in this project are : raw materials (eg. Wax, Resin, PVA, PIB, Butyl, Polyols), packaging (eg. Tin, Plastic jars, fiber-based packaging, labels), MRO (Maintenance, Repair and Operations: eg. Rotors, Rotary Equiqment), office supplies, marketing, transportation and energy. The product category relation *product-Category* is generated to cater for this functional requirement as shown below:

```
productCategory(?id, ?category).
```

The structural product category facts are captured in RuleML syntax as shown in Appendix C, Listing 5 Lines: 111-152.

4.2.4   Knowledge Design: Rules

The ontology-based structural facts in the KB explained in Section 4.2.1 and Section 4.2.3 examines the main functionalities that have been implemented. The policy rules are implemented in the knowledge base using RuleML syntax to deduce some meaning whiles the query process employs the POSL syntax because of compactness of the snytax. The details both policy rules and RuleML syntax are represented below to illustrate the policies in the Section 4.1.

Search Rule Syntax Representation

- *getProductCategory (?ID, ?productCategory) ← productCategory(?ID, ?productCategory).*

- *getProduct(?id, ?name, ?code, ?price, ?att, ?quantity, ?man, ?supplier, ?description, ?category) ← product(?id, ?name, ?code, ?price, ?att, ?quantity, ?man, ?supplier, ?description, ?category).*

- *requestQuote(?id, ?bod, ?actor, ?location, ?requestDate, ?relatedTo) ← supplier(?name, ?description, ?transport, ?telephone, ?city, ?webpage, ?role) ∧ product(?id, ?name, ?code, ?price, ?att, ?quantity, ?man, ?supplier, ?description, ?category).*

Supplier Refund Policy Syntax Representation

- *(Rule B:) getReFund(?client, ?product, ?year) ← refund(?client, fullpurchase) ∧ returnGood(?client, ?product, defective) ∧ dateDiff(?year, now, comYear, 1).*

Three structural knowledge base facts are required for this policy rule:

```
refund(?client, fullpurchase).
returnGood(?client, ?product, defective).
dateDiff(?year, now, comYear, 1).
```

The dateDiff(?year, now, comYear, 1) is a builtin function in the OO jDREW. The detail representation in RuleML is shown in Appendix C,Listing 5.

Supplier Discount Policy Syntax Representation

The supplier discount policy in Example 4.1.2 gives five policy rules expressed using the policy rule in LT-Policy.

- (Rule A:) *getDiscount(?client, ?supplier, 5) ← loyalCustomer(?client, ?supplier) ∧ actionHistory(payment-evt, ?client, ?paymentAction, ?bod, ?activityDate).*

- (Rule B:) *getDiscount(?client, ?supplier, 10) ← bigSpender(?client, ?supplier) ∧ actionHistory(payment-evt, ?client, ?paymentAction, ?bod, ?activityDate).*

- (Rule C:) *getDiscount(?client, 5) ← hasCard(?client, ProviderCard).*

- (Rule D:) *getDiscount(?client, 10) ← memberOf(?client, PlatinumClub).*

- (Rule E:) *getDiscount(?client, 0) ← actionHistory(latePayment, ?client, ?paymentAction, ?bod, ?activityDate) ∧ dateDiff(?activityDate, now, comYear, 1).*

These facts are represented in the KB:

```
loyalCustomer(?client, ?supplier).
bigSpender(?client, ?supplier).
hasCard(?client, ProviderCard).
memberOf(?client, PlatinumClub).
```

The detail representation in RuleML is shown in Appendix C,Listing 5.

Warranty Policy Syntax Representation

The warranty discount policy in Example 4.1.3 gives two policy rules expressed using the policy rule in LT-Policy as:

- (Rule A:) getWarranty(?id, ?years, ?category) ← warranty(?id, ?years) ∧ productCategory(?id, ?category).
  warranty(?id, ?years) is the fact in the knowledge base and is based on the category of the product catalog.

- (Rule B:) getWarranty(?years) ← warranty(?years).

This fact is represented in RuleML syntax and added to the KB.

```
warranty(?category, ?years) %Warranty Fact in KB
```

The detail representation in RuleML is shown in Appendix C,Listing 5: Lines 192-212.

Authorization Policy Syntax Representation

The following policy rules formulated in $C3$ are repeated just for the sole purpose of the syntax representation:

- (Rule A): $\forall (s_1, a_1, r_1, l_1, t_1) \in \mathcal{SARLT}$: authorized$(s_1, a_1, r_1, l_1, t_1) \leftarrow$ permission$(s_1, a_1, r_1, l_1, t_1) \wedge$ enact(a_1, l_1, t_1).

- (Rule B): $\forall (s_2, a_2, r_2, l_2, t_2) \in \mathcal{SARLT}$: authorized$(s_2, a_2, r_2, l_2, t_2) \leftarrow$ permission$(s_2, a_2, r_2, l_2, t_2) \wedge$ enact(a_2, l_2, t_2).

The representation of the authorization policy syntax is in Appendix B, Listing 3.

Chapter 5

E-Procurement Prototype and its Evaluation on the knowledge Base

The use of policy can be an effective mechanism to allows users to take control of their private information in an open and dynamic environment. The Semantic Web languages such as OWL and RDF/RDFS are suitable languages for defining new policy languages because of their expressive power and support for knowledge representation and reasoning and knowledge sharing and integration.

5.1 Adaptation of the Rule Engine: OO jDREW

In this section, I will describe the rule engine OO jDREW, which serves as a tool for RuleML. Mandarax [32], Prova [33], SweetRules [34] and jDREW [35] have also been developed as rule engines supporting various subsets of RuleML. OO jDREW provides a reasoning engine to make it easier to reason about the details of an access request, and about the context in which access requests are evaluated. OO jDREW has two modes of operations: OO jDREW BU (Bottom Up) and OO jDREW TD (Top Down).

OO jDREW TD: In OO jDREW Top Down, rules are used to answer queries by reducing them to subqueries until facts are reached. Three features are designed in OO jDREW TD:

- Type Definition, realized in RDFS and POSL syntax, which comprises the subClassOf taxonomy: type hierarchy for the users KB.

- KB, which stores the fact and rules, as in OO jDREW BU, for query on demand.

- Querying the KB, either in RuleML or POSL syntax.

The features has proved to be enough for the implementation of the policy reasoning.

5.1.1 Contributions to OO jDREW

RDFS Parser Problem. The *RDFSParser* class of OO jDREW was not capable of parsing the e-Procurement ontology designed with Protege. The *parseClass* method of the RDFSParser class was re-implemented to support the parser problem identified and the details of the method is shown in Appendix A, Listing 1.

Types. The *createDAGNode* method of the *Types* class is minorly edited to prevent the method throwing exceptions if a particular type is already present in the temporary store which is not suitable for this work. The details of the method is shown in Appendix A, Listing 2.

5.2 Evaluation of Knowledge Base: Semantic e-Procurement Prototype

The E-Procurement prototype is made up of three basic operations namely:

- Searchable Facts
- Sourcing System
- Policy Rule

Figure 5.1 shows the logical view of interaction in the prototype been exhibited here. The prototype is built on top of the rule engine, OO jDREW. This project is focused on knowledge acquisition in procurement domain and application of policies/rules on the KB. First, the user posts a query to the E-Procurement prototype via OO jDREW Graphical User Interface. The E-Procurement prototype then automatically applies the corresponding rules to the related procurement domain facts. After processing facts with rules and ontology definitions, the result of the E-Procurement rule system may turn out be either a success or a failure. The queries that are deducible from the knowledge base is represented as a result bindings. Otherwise, "No Solution" shows up in the result binding view on the left column of the OO jDREW GUI Query TabView.

5.2.1 Core functionality of E-Procurement Sourcing Prototype

The functional operations of e-procurement prototype are:

1. Searching for a particular product or product category.

2. Searching for a supplier for a particular product or category.

3. Searching for authorized procurement actions or processes in the KB.

4. Generate a workflow of an activity in the procurement process.

5. Verification of policy rules with the knowledge base.

5.2.2 OO jDREW TD UI: Running the prototype

The E-Procurement prototype is executed using the built-in OO jDREW TD UI (cf. Figure 5.2). The basic steps for running the prototype are:

1. Load the RDFS type definition (by copying Appendix C, Listing 6 and click on the "Load Type Information" button) in the Type Definition Tab.

2. Click on the "Show Debug Console" to check for errors during the parsing process.

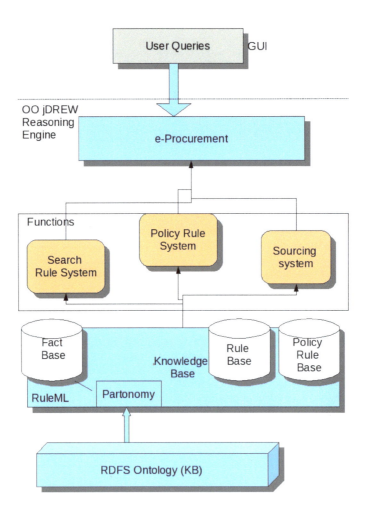

Figure 5.1: E-Procurement Logical View

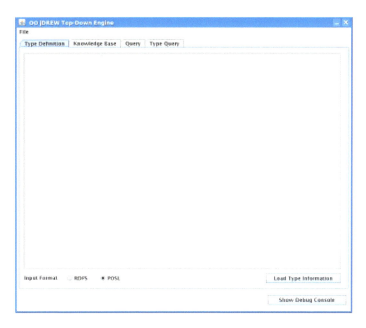

Figure 5.2: Screen Shot: GUI of the Top Down Engine

3. Load the RuleML (check RuleML 0.91) KB details into the input field by copying the content of Appendix C, Listing 5 the Knowledge Base Tab and parse the knowledge base.

4. Click on the "Show Debug Console" to check for errors during the parsing process.

5. Issue your RuleML/POSL queries in the upperbox field in the Query Tab.

6. Click on the "Issue Query" button to execute the query.

7. After the query computation is complete, result bindings will be shown on the right-hand side of the interface. Use the "Next Solution" button to navigate through the solutions provided, if it is enabled.

5.2.3 Experimental View of the prototype.

In this section, the E-Procurement prototype is tested under basic operations using varying types of different queries. Each of the subdomains are tested as separate module at first, and then together as a whole system, in order to verify the system operations. The following examples are used to illustrate the typical operations in the prototype.

Search Operations

Here, the basic search operations with the knowledge base is illustrated as to how the representations of information in the knowledge base with the RuleML syntax is queried using the deductive reasoning engine, Object-Oriented jDREW. Mainly queries for product

Figure 5.3: Screenshot of Product Category Result for Query 1

categories, product details, supplier details, etc are exhibited to conceptualize the semantic e-prcourement prototype.

Search for Product Categories The first query in Table 5.1 returns a unique solution as it queries for product category details. The system binds the detailed information of the unifying product category to the free variables "?id" and "?category" as shown in Figure 5.3.

Table 5.1: Queries for different inputs for the product category search.

Query	User Input	Query Snytax
1	None	getProductCategory(?id:ID, ?category:ProductAtt)
2	**?id**	getProductCategory(**?id**:ID, ?category:ProductAtt)
3	**?category**	getProductCategory(?id:ID, **?category**:ProductAtt)

Query 1: This is similar to the SQL query, *select * from productCategory*. This generates all the product categories in the KB. The expected result count of this query is 8.

Query 2: This query returns the unique product category based on the supplied value of the variable, "?id". The variable "?id" is replaced in the second query by any value in Table 5.1 and the resultant variable is shown in the left side of Table 5.2. For example, if the variable, **?id** is 2 then the ?category variable is binded to **packaging**.

Query 3: The third query searches for a unique identifier based on the supplied information of the product category. The result bindings show similar result as shown in Table 5.2. For example, if **?category** is **raw material** then the KB binds the variable, **?id** to a value of **1** after the unification process.

Search for Products

Query 1: getProduct(?prod: ProductID, ?name: ProductName, ?uprice: UnitPrice, ?quant: ProductQuantity, ?man: Manufacturer, ?desc: Description; supplierID− > ?sid:ID; productCategoryID− > ?cid:ID).
This first query queries the knowledge base for all registered products in the knowledge base. Details result of the query can be found as shown in Figure 5.4

Table 5.2: Product category result for Query 2.

?id	Variable Bindings	
	Variable	Binding
1	?category:ProductAtt	"raw material":ProductAtt
2	?category:ProductAtt	"packaging":ProductAtt
3	?category:ProductAtt	"material and services":ProductAtt
4	?category:ProductAtt	"office supplies":ProductAtt
5	?category:ProductAtt	"marketing":ProductAtt
6	?category:ProductAtt	"transportation":ProductAtt
7	?category:ProductAtt	"energy":ProductAtt
8	?category:ProductAtt	"MRO":ProductAtt

Query 2: getProduct(?prod: ProductID, ?name: ProductName, ?uprice: UnitPrice, ?quant: ProductQuantity, ?man: Manufacturer, ?desc: Description; supplierID− > ?sid:ID; productCategoryID− > **?cid**:ID).

The query result with a user input of 3 for the logical variable, **?cid** shows the result in the Table 5.3.

Figure 5.4: Result for searching all the products in the knowledge base

Table 5.3: Product Search Result with ?cid=3 using query 2.

?cid	Variable Bindings	
	Variable	Binding
3	?desc:Description	"Viking Plastic Box File Black.":Description
	?sid : ID	"s-133339" : ID
	?uprice : UnitPrice	4.19 : UnitPrice
	?prod : ProductID	s007 : ProductID
	?quant : ProductQuantity	1450 : ProductQuantity
	?name : ProductName	"Box Files" : ProductName
	?man : Manufacturer	Viking : Manufacturer

Search for Suppliers   The key actor in the procurement sourcing process is the supplier. The supplier may be referred to as a francished delear, distributor, wholesaler, merchant or manufacturer. There are four different forms of query that can be performed on the

Figure 5.5: Supplier list search in the Knowledge Base.

Figure 5.6: Supplier Information Search Result

supplier information, mainly searching for supplier company information, supplier contact person, supplier profile and supplier product category-based.

Query 1 supplier(companyInfo $-$ > [?ciid:ID, ?companyName:Company, ?desc:Description, ?city:City, ?country:Country, ?comtel:TelePhone, ?page:URI, ?ciemail:Email]; contactPerson $-$ > [?cname:ContactName, ?job:JobTitle, ?tel:TelePhone, ?cemail:Email]; companyProfile $-$ > [productCategory$-$ >?cid:ID; ?lob:LOB, ?mode:TransportMode, ?role:Actor])
Figure 5.5 shows the result of this query.

Query 2 getSupplierCompanyInfo(companyInfo $-$ > [?ciid:ID, ?companyName: Company, ?desc: Description, ?city:City, ?country:Country, ?comtel:TelePhone, ?page:URI, ?ciemail: Email]).
Figure 5.6 shows the result of this query.

Search for Workflow A workflow is a model to represent real work for further assessment and the focus here is in the procurement domain. The first query in Table 5.4 returns a unique solution as it queries for process workflow details. The system binds the detailed information of the unifying process workflow to the free variables "?process" and "?subProcess" as shown in Figure 5.7. The second query searches for specific sub-processes of a process. The valid values for this logical variable "?process" are order, despatch, invoice and source. Figure 5.8 and Table 5.5 shows the result for the sequence of operation for the **order** process.

Table 5.4: Queries for different inputs for the process workflow search.

Query	User Input	Query Snytax
1	None	getPartOfProcess(?process, ?subProcess)
2	**?process**	getPartOfProcess(**?process**, ?subProcess)

Query 1: This query returns all the process workflows in the KB.

Query 2: This query returns all the sub-processes of the value of the variable, **?process**. In SQL sense, this query can be described as select all the sub-processes where the process=**?process**. It is a depiction of a sequence of operations to acheive a particular business process.

Figure 5.7: Process Workflow Result for Query 1

Figure 5.8: Process Workflow result for Query 2

Search for Platinum Club Members Members of the platinum club are distinguished clients for the supplier. These details provide the supplier information about members and

Table 5.5: Process Workflow result for Query 2.

?process	Variable Bindings	
	Variable	Binding
order	?subprocess	issuePO
	?subprocess	issuePO
	?subprocess	responsePO
	?subprocess	requestPOChange
	?subprocess	changePO

this information is used by the supplier to calculate discount rates for it's members during their purchasing business process. The queries in Table 5.6 shows the possible searches that can be made. Generally, all variables search query, search by client query and search by card name query.

Table 5.6: Queries for different inputs for the Platinum Club Member search.

Query	User Input	Query Snytax
1	None	getPlatinumMember(?client:Client, ?club)
2	**?client**	getPlatinumMember(**?client**:Client, ?club)
3	**?club**	getPlatinumMember(?client:Client, **?club**)

Search for Provider Card Holders   The discount policy rule makes use of this provider card holders information and it serves the same purpose as the platinum club members. Sample possible queries with the knowledge base can be found in Table 5.7.

Table 5.7: Queries for different inputs for the provider card holder search.

Query	User Input	Query Snytax
1	None	getProviderCardHolder(?client, ?card)
2	**?client**	getProviderCardHolder(**?client**, ?card)
3	**?card**	getProviderCardHolder(?client, **?card**)

Search for Action History

Query 1 getActionHistory(?event, ?client:Payee, ?action:Action, ?res:Entity; time− > [startTime− > ?t1:Date; endTime− >?t2:Date]).

Query 2 getActionHistory(payment-evt, ?client:Payee, ?action:Action, ?res:Entity; time− > [startTime− > ?t1:Date; endTime− > ?t2:Date]).

The first query searches for all actions that has occurred and has been recorded in the knowledge base. A sample action history result is shown in Figure 5.9. The second query is more specific for all action histories for the event **payment-evt** and the result variable binding is shown in Table 5.8.

Figure 5.9: Action history results in the knowledge base for Query 1

Table 5.8: Action History variable binding for Query 2.

?event	Variable Bindings	
	Variable	Binding
payment-evt	?client:Payee	client-111:Payee
	?t2:Date	"13/04/2010:1300PM":Date
	?t1 : Date	"13/04/2010:1200AM":Date
	?action:Action	payment-action:Action
	?res:Entity	PVA:Entity

Verification of Business Policies

This section provides analysis of the policy rules in Section 4.2.4 with the knowledge acquisition represented in the knowledge base as modeled information with the domain concepts in RDFS.

Warranty Policy   A warranty is an assurance, promise, or guaranty by one party that a particular statement of fact is true and may be relied upon by the other party. This warranty policies expresses the fact that certain product categories have some t-year warranty for any product that falls in that particular category where t can be either weeks, months or years. Table 5.9 contains all the possible queries that are valid to work with the KB.

Table 5.9: Queries for different inputs for the warranty policy.

Query	User Input	Query Snytax
1	None	getWarranty(?id:ID, ?year:Year, ?categoryName:ProductAtt)
2	**?id**	getWarranty(**?id**:ID, ?year:Year, ?categoryName:ProductAtt)
3	**?year**	getWarranty(?id:ID, **?year**:Year, ?categoryName:ProductAtt)
4	**?categoryName**	getWarranty(?id:ID, ?year:Year, **?categoryName**:ProductAtt)

Query 1: In similar search process, the first query provides a search for all warranty facts in the knowledge base. The three variables specifically the product category unique identifier, the years of warranty and the product category which are provided by the *productCategory* relation are binded to the knowledge information during the

unification process. The type definitions of the variables are resolved if they match with the RDFS defintions then the reasoning engine returns the result bindings as shown in Figure 5.10.

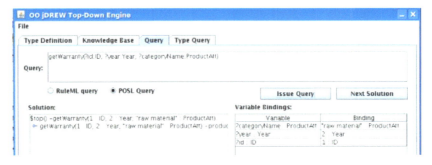

Figure 5.10: Warranty Policy Result for Query 1

Query 2: The second query searches for a warrant guarantee for a product category based on the the variable, **?id**. With this query only a single result binding is achieved because this is a specific query with a *where* clause if we are taking sides with SQL statements. The sample result is shown in Figure 5.11.

Discount Policy The discount policy is based mainly on four criteria namely clients that are big spenders, clients/customers that are loyal, clients that are member of the supplier's platinum club and clients that are holders of the provider card. The suppliers discount rate is either 5 percent or 10 percent of the client's total spending cost. The five sample queries in Table 5.10 are explained below.

Table 5.10: Queries for different inputs for the discount policy.

Query	User Input	Query Snytax
1	None	getDiscount(?client:Client, 10:DiscountPercent)
2	**?client**	getDiscount(**?client**:Client, ?discount:DiscountPercent)
3	None	getDiscount(?client, ?discount:DiscountPercent)
4	None	getDiscount(?client, 5:DiscountPercent)
5	None	getDiscount(?c:Payee, ?s:Manufacturer, ?dis:DiscountPercent)

Figure 5.11: Warrany Policy Result for Query 2

Query 1: This query does not required any input from the user. It returns all the clients that are eligible for a 10 percent discount on their total spendings. Figure 5.12 illustrates the result of the POSL query in the reasoning engine. This discount policy is deduced from the *memberOf* relation associated with the platinum club of the supplier.

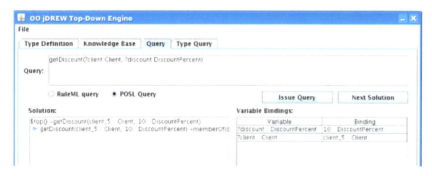

Figure 5.12: Discount Policy(Platinum Club Member) Result for Query 1

Query 2: This second query rather searches for a discount that an eligible client is entitled to with its supplier. The user's input is the client whom the discount is being searched for in the knowledge base. The result of the search query is shown in Figure 5.13. The user should iterate through the solution with the "Next Solution" button if it is visible.

Figure 5.13: Discount Policy(Platinum Club Member) Result for Query 2

Query 3: The third query requires no input from the user. The third query searches for all discounts with the associated clients. This information can be used by the discount policy rule to deduce discounts for card holders. Figure 5.14 provides an iterativable solution of the deducible results from the knowledge base. The deducible result is based on the provider card holder facts in the database.

Query 4: This query is rather simple because it just searches for all clients that are eligible for a discount of 5 percent. Figure 5.15 shows the result of the query after running through the knowledge base and the variable bindings are unified by the reasoning engine. This query is based on the *hasCard* relationship and the deduction process is via that relationship.

Figure 5.14: Discount Policy(Provider Card Holder) Result for Query 2

Figure 5.15: Discount Policy(Provider Card Holder) Result for Query 1

Query 5: A discount can also be given to clients that have a history of big spending with its supplier. The conditions for a client to be eligible for a discount is depend on the fact that the client is recorded in the supplier's database as a big spender and more importantly, there is a payment history with details of payment transaction like payment date, business object document (entity) etc. The client is playing a role of a Payee in this discount policy rule. This query searches for all clients that are eligible for a 10 percent discount. The result variable bindigs of the query is shown in Figure 5.16.

Figure 5.16: Discount Policy (Big Spender and Payment History Conditions) Result for Query 5

Figure 5.17: Authorization Policy Rule Search

Verification of Authorization Policy Rule

This is to verify the possible authorization policy rules in the knowledge base. The first query produces the result as shown in Figure 5.17. It took 33ms to resolve the binding with a knowledge base of 3 *permissions* and *enact* facts. These rules come to play during the exchange of business policy rules with different agents. In order to build trust with the agents, they must authenticate and authorize their activities to ensure identity and rights of agents. This just illustrates how the authorization information is deduced by the reasoning engine during a practical agent-to-agent interaction. A typical query like Query 2, check if an agent is capable to issue a quote for client say "client-5".

Query 1 authorized(?subject:Actor, ?act:Action, ?ent:Entity, ?place:Place; time $->$ [startTime $->$?start:Date; endTime $->$?end:Date]).

Query 2 authorized(client-5:Actor, issueQuote:Action, ?ent:Entity, ?place:Place; time $->$ [startTime $->$?start:Date; endTime $->$?end:Date]).

System Setup

The testing of the E-Procurement prototype was done in the linux platform with the specification as shown in Table 5.11. On average, it takes about 16 milliseconds for a

Table 5.11: Specification of Setup System.

Property Name	Property Value
Operating System (os)	Linux Fedora Core 8
Java Runtime Engine	1.6.0 Update 13
Maximum Memory Avaliable	512MB
os.arch	i586

typical search query on the knowledge base. The knowledge base is too big but much in appreciable size to illustrate the evaluation of the system.

Chapter 6

Conclusion

There are several extensions that I will consider. One concerns the enforcement of authorisation and authentication – the authentication system is pluggable primarily through providing custom *LoginModule* implementations, while the authorization system is pluggable by providing both custom *java.security.Permission* implementations, and *java.security.Policy* implementations. The JAAS[1] framework provides the building blocks to enforce the authentication and authorisation policies. This project focused only on the process of policy rules but one could look at the exchange of knowledge, policy rules and negotiation about their meanings. The modeled access control policy is much brought to light during the exchange process with agents with the aim to access that the activities of the agents are authenticated and authorized. The Rule Responder[2] is an initiative which is exploring this area of research but the context of this project can be examined for some possibilities:

- Storing, deconflicting, and querying through the Repository Service.
- Distribution of policies to Policy Decision Point(PDP).
- Implementation of policies through Policy Enforcers.
- Policy disclosure through Policy Query Interface.
- Policy versioning
- History Monitors
- Services Interface: Transport, Registration, Request, Query, Subcribe.

---

[1] Java Authentication and Authorisation Service (JAAS) : `http://download-llnw.oracle.com/javase/6/docs/technotes/guides/security/jaas/JAASRefGuide.html`

[2] Rule Responder : `http://ibis.in.tum.de/projects/paw/`

Bibliography

[1] Michael Kifer. Rule Interchange Format: The Framework, 2008.

[2] RuleML, The Rule Markup Initiative. `http://ruleml.org/` (Accessed March 24, 2010).

[3] Joseph Y. Halpern and Vicky Weissman. Using First-Order Logic to Reason about Policies, 2006.

[4] G. Governatori, J. Hall, and A. Paschke (Eds.). Geospatial-Enabled RuleML in a Study on Querying Respiratory Disease Information: RuleML 2009. LNCS 5858, pp. 272-281. Springer-Verlag Berlin Heidelberg 2009.

[5] Marcel Ball, Harold Boley, David Hirtle1, Jing Mei1, and Bruce Spencer. The OO jDREW Reference Implementation of RuleML A. Adi et al. (Eds.): RuleML 2005, LNCS 3791, pp. 218-223.Springer-Verlag Berlin Heidelberg 2005

[6] Guido Governatori and Antonino Rotolo. 'Modelling Contracts Using RuleML' in T. Gordon (ed.) Legal Knowledge and Information Systems. Jurix 2004: The Seventeenth Annual Conference. Amsterdam IOS Press, 2004, pp. 141-150.

[7] OO jDREW. `http://www.jdrew.org/oojdrew/` (Accessed March 25, 2010).

[8] Pling, w3c policy languages interest group (Accessed April 02, 2010). `http://www.w3.org/Policy/pling/`

[9] SAML (2010), `http://xml.coverpages.org/saml.html` (Accessed April 02, 2010)

[10] P3P, `http://www.w3.org/P3P/` (Accessed April 02, 2010)

[11] XACML, Extensible Access Control Markup Language, Web Page: `http://xml.coverpages.org/xacml.html`

[12] H. Boley, S. Taber, and G. Wagner. Design Rationale of RuleML: A Markup Language for Semantic Web Rules. Proc. SWWS01, Stanford, July/August 2001.

[13] G. Wagner. How to Design a General Rule Markup Language. Eindhoven University of Technology, Faculty of Technology Management, June 2002.

[14] Harold Boley. Object-Oriented RuleML:User-Level Roles, URI-Grounded Clauses, and Order-Sorted Terms, 2004.

[15] Ora Lassila and Ralph R. Swick. Resource Description Framework (RDF) Model and Syntax Specification. Recommendation REC-rdf-syntax-19990222, W3C, February 1999.

[16] Noy, N. F. and McGuinness, D. L. Ontology development 101 : A guide to creating your first ontology, Web Page: `http://protege.stanford.edu/publications/` (Accessed April 04, 2010).

[17] W3C: OWL Web Ontology Language Reference. Web page: `http://www.w3.org/TR/owlref/` (Accessed April 28,2010).

[18] Protégé Project. Web page: `http://protege.stanford.edu` (Accessed April 28,2010).

[19] Y Venema. Temporal Logic,in: L Goble (editor), The Blackwell Guide to Philosophical Logic. Blackwell Publishers, Malden, USA, 2001, pp 203 - 223.

[20] Gianluca Tonti, Jeffrey M. Bradshaw, Renia Jeffers, Rebecca Montanari, Niranjan Suri, and Andrzej Uszok. Semantic Web Languages for Policy Representation and Reasoning: A Comparison of KAoS, Rei, and Ponder. Springer-Verlag Berlin Heidelberg, 2003, pp 419-437.

[21] Berthold Daum. Modeling Business Objects with XML Schema. Morgan Kaufmann Publishers 2003.

[22] Kristof Van Belleghem, Marc Denecker, and Danny De Schreye, On The Relation Between Situation Calculus And Event Calculus. Elsevier Science Inc., 1997.

[23] Maedche, A. Ontology Learning for the Sematic Web. Kluwer Academic Publishers, 2002.

[24] Antonio De Nicola, Michele Missikoff and Roberto Navigli. A software engineering approach to ontology building. July 2008. Elsevier B. V.

[25] Foundations of Inductive Logic Programming. Logic. Springer Berlin/ Heidelberg, 1997, pp 35-53.

[26] WS-BPEL. `http://www.oasis-open.org/committees/tc_home.php?wg_abbrev=wsbpel`. 2010.

[27] J. Biskup and J. Lopez. A Policy Language for Distributed Usage Control (Eds.), ESORICS 2007, LNCS 4734, pp. 531546, 2007. Springer-Verlag Berlin Heidelberg 2007.

[28] Jaehong Park and Ravi Sandhu. The $UCON_{ABC}$ Usage Control Model. ACM Transactions on Information and System Security, Vol. 7, No. 1, February 2004, Pages 128174.

[29] Benjamin N. Grosof, Yannis Labrou and Hoi Y. Chan. A Declarative Approach to Business Rules in Contracts: Courteous Logic Programs in XML. ACM Conference on Electronic Commerce (EC99), Denver, Colorado, USA, Nov. 35, 1999.

[30] Michael Kifer, George Lausen, and James Wu. Logic Foundations of Object Oriented and Frame Based Languages, Journal of the Association for Computing Machinary, 1995.

[31] Harold Boley. Integrating positional and slotted knowledge on the semantic web, `http://www.ruleml.org/posl/poslintweb-talk.pdf`, March 2005.

[32] Mandarax. `http://mandarax.sourceforge.net/`.

[33] Prova Language. `http://comas.soi.city.ac.uk/prova`.

[34] SweetRules. `http://sweetrules.projects.semwebcentral.org/`.

[35] jDREW. `http://www.jrew.org`.

[36] Guido Boella, Joris Hulstijn, and Leendert van der Torre. Argumentation for Access Control. Springer-Verlag Berlin Heidelberg 2005.AI*IA 2005, LNAI 3673, pp. 8697, 2005.

[37] Ravi S. Sandhu and Pierangela Samarati. Access Control: Principles and Practise. IEEE Communications Magazine, September 1994.

Appendix A: Source Codes

Listing 1: parseClass method of the RDFSParser class

```
1  private static void parseClass(Element cls) {
2  String typename = cls.getAttributeValue(ID, rdfuri);
3  if (typename == null) {
4  typename = cls.getAttributeValue(ABOUT, rdfuri);
5  if (typename == null) {
6  return; }
7  }
8  if (typename.indexOf("#") > 0) {
9  typename = typename.substring(typename.indexOf("#") + 1);
10 }
11 Vector v = new Vector();
12 Elements els = cls.getChildElements();
13 for (int i = 0; i < els.size(); i++) {
14 Element el = els.get(i);
15 if (el.getQualifiedName().equals(RDFSSUBCLASSOF)) {
16 String parentname = el.getAttributeValue(RESOURCE, rdfuri);
17 if (parentname == null) {
18 Element subEls = el.getChildElements().get(0);
19 parseClass(subEls);
20 if (subEls.getQualifiedName().equals(RDFSCLASS)) {
21 parentname = subEls.getAttributeValue(ID, rdfuri);
22 if (parentname == null) {
23 parentname = subEls.getAttributeValue(ABOUT, rdfuri); } } }
24 if (parentname.indexOf("#") >= 0) {
25 parentname = parentname.substring(parentname.indexOf("#") + 1); }
26 v.add(parentname); } }
27 String[] parents = new String[v.size()];
28 String parentstr = "";
29 for (int i = 0; i < parents.length; i++) {
30 parents[i] = v.get(i).toString();
31 parentstr += v.get(i).toString() + " ";}
32 logger.info("Creating Type: " + typename + " parents: " + parentstr);
33 Types.storeTempTypes(typename, parents);
34 }
```

Listing 2: createDAGNode method of the Types class

```
1  public static int createDAGNode(String name) {
2  if (types.contains(name)) {
3  log.warn("Type " + name +
4  " already exists, cannot create type definition.");
5  return 0; }
6  int id = types.size();
7  types.add(name);
8  Integer iID = new Integer(id);
9  dag.addNodeWeight(iID);
10 return id;
11 }
```

Appendix B: Policy Rule Sets

Listing 3: E-Procurement Rules

```
1  <!-- Authorization Rule -->
2  <Implies>
3  <!-- body -->
4  <And>
5          <Atom>
6                  <Rel>permission</Rel>
7                  <Var type="Actor">subject</Var>
8                  <Var type="Action">action</Var>
9                  <Var type="Entity">resource</Var>
10                 <Var type="Place">location</Var>
11          <slot>
12                  <Ind>time</Ind>
13                  <Plex>
14                  <slot>
15                  <Ind>startTime</Ind>
16                  <Var type="Date">t1</Var>
17                  </slot>
18                  <slot>
19                  <Ind>endTime</Ind>
20                  <Var type="Date">t2</Var>
21                  </slot>
22                  </Plex>
23              </slot>
24          </Atom>
25          <Atom>
26                  <Rel>enact</Rel>
27                  <Var type="Action">action</Var>
28                  <Var type="Place">location</Var>
29          <slot>
30                  <Ind>time</Ind>
31                  <Plex>
32                  <slot>
33                  <Ind>startTime</Ind>
34                  <Var type="Date">t1</Var>
35                  </slot>
36                  <slot>
37                  <Ind>endTime</Ind>
38                  <Var type="Date">t2</Var>
39                  </slot>
40                  </Plex>
41              </slot>
42          </Atom>
43  </And>
44  <!-- head -->
45          <Atom>
46                  <Rel>authorized</Rel>
47                  <Var type="Actor">subject</Var>
48                  <Var type="Action">action</Var>
49                  <Var type="Entity">resource</Var>
50                  <Var type="Place">location</Var>
51          <slot>
52                  <Ind>time</Ind>
```

```
53              <Plex>
54              <slot>
55              <Ind>startTime</Ind>
56              <Var type="Date">t1</Var>
57              </slot>
58              <slot>
59              <Ind>endTime</Ind>
60              <Var type="Date">t2</Var>
61              </slot>
62              </Plex>
63          </slot>
64      </Atom>
65  </Implies>
66  <Implies>
67  <!-- body Prohibition -->
68  <And>
69      <Atom>
70          <Rel>prohibition</Rel>
71          <Var type="Actor">subject</Var>
72          <Var type="Action">action</Var>
73          <Var type="Entity">resource</Var>
74          <Var type="Place">location</Var>
75          <slot>
76          <Ind>time</Ind>
77          <Plex>
78          <slot>
79          <Ind>startTime</Ind>
80          <Var type="Date">t1</Var>
81          </slot>
82          <slot>
83          <Ind>endTime</Ind>
84          <Var type="Date">t2</Var>
85          </slot>
86          </Plex>
87          </slot>
88      </Atom>
89      <Atom>
90          <Rel>disenact</Rel>
91          <Var type="Action">action</Var>
92          <Var type="Place">location</Var>
93          <slot>
94          <Ind>time</Ind>
95          <Plex>
96          <slot>
97          <Ind>startTime</Ind>
98          <Var type="Date">t1</Var>
99          </slot>
100         <slot>
101         <Ind>endTime</Ind>
102         <Var type="Date">t2</Var>
103         </slot>
104         </Plex>
105         </slot>
106     </Atom>
107 </And>
```

```
108   <!-- head -->
109   <Neg>
110           <Atom>
111                   <Rel>authorized</Rel>
112                   <Var type="Actor">subject</Var>
113                   <Var type="Action">action</Var>
114                   <Var type="Entity">resource</Var>
115                   <Var type="Place">location</Var>
116             <slot>
117                   <Ind>time</Ind>
118                   <Plex>
119                   <slot>
120                   <Ind>startTime</Ind>
121                   <Var type="Date">t1</Var>
122                   </slot>
123                   <slot>
124                   <Ind>endTime</Ind>
125                   <Var type="Date">t2</Var>
126                   </slot>
127                   </Plex>
128               </slot>
129           </Atom>
130   </Neg>
131   </Implies>
132           <!-- Partonomy Rule -->
133   <Implies>
134                   <!--<body>-->
135           <Atom>
136                   <Rel>partOfProcess</Rel>
137                   <Var>process</Var>
138                   <Var>subprocess</Var>
139           </Atom>
140                   <!--<head>-->
141           <Atom>
142                   <Rel>getPartOfProcess</Rel>
143                   <Var>process</Var>
144                   <Var>subprocess</Var>
145           </Atom>
146   </Implies>
147   <!-- Product Category Rule -->
148   <Implies>
149           <!-- Body -->
150           <Atom>
151           <Rel>productCategory</Rel>
152           <Var type="ID">productID</Var>
153           <Var type="ProductAtt">productCategory</Var>
154           </Atom>
155           <!-- Head -->
156           <Atom>
157           <Rel>getProductCategory</Rel>
158           <Var type="ID">productID</Var>
159           <Var type="ProductAtt">productCategory</Var>
160           </Atom>
161   </Implies>
162   <Implies>
```

```xml
163          <!-- body -->
164          <Atom>
165                  <Rel>memberOf</Rel>
166                  <Var>client</Var>
167                  <Ind>PlatinumClub</Ind>
168          </Atom>
169          <!-- head -->
170          <Atom>
171                  <Rel>getDiscount</Rel>
172                  <Var>client</Var>
173                  <Ind type="DiscountPercent">10</Ind>
174          </Atom>
175  </Implies>
176  <Implies>
177          <!-- body -->
178          <Atom>
179                  <Rel>memberOf</Rel>
180                  <Var>client</Var>
181                  <Ind>PlatinumClub</Ind>
182          </Atom>
183          <!-- head -->
184          <Atom>
185                  <Rel>getDiscount</Rel>
186                  <Var>client</Var>
187                  <Ind type="DiscountPercent">10</Ind>
188          </Atom>
189  </Implies>
190  <!-- Warranty Rule -->
191  <Implies>
192          <!-- body -->
193          <And>
194                  <Atom>
195                  <Rel>productCategory</Rel>
196                  <Var type="ID">catID</Var>
197                  <Var type="ProductAtt">category</Var>
198                  </Atom>
199                  <Atom>
200                  <Rel>warranty</Rel>
201                  <Var type="ID">catID</Var>
202                  <Var type="Year">years</Var>
203                  </Atom>
204          </And>
205  <!-- head -->
206          <Atom>
207          <Rel>getWarranty</Rel>
208          <Var type="ID">catID</Var>
209          <Var type="Year">years</Var>
210          <Var type="ProductAtt">category</Var>
211          </Atom>
212  </Implies>
213  <!-- Product Search Rule -->
214  <Implies>
215          <!-- Body -->
216          <Atom>
217                  <Rel>product</Rel>
```

```
218              <Var type="ProductID">prodID</Var>
219              <Var type="ProductName">name</Var>
220              <Var type="UnitPrice">uprice</Var>
221              <Var type="ProductQuantity">quant</Var>
222              <Var type="Manufacturer">manufac</Var>
223              <Var type="Description">desc</Var>
224          <slot>
225              <Ind>supplierID</Ind>
226              <Var type="ID">sid</Var>
227          </slot>
228          <slot>
229              <Ind>productCategoryID</Ind>
230              <Var type="ID">pid</Var>
231          </slot>
232      </Atom>
233      <!-- Head -->
234      <Atom>
235              <Rel>getProduct</Rel>
236              <Var type="ProductID">prodID</Var>
237              <Var type="ProductName">name</Var>
238              <Var type="UnitPrice">uprice</Var>
239              <Var type="ProductQuantity">quant</Var>
240              <Var type="Manufacturer">manufac</Var>
241              <Var type="Description">desc</Var>
242          <slot>
243              <Ind>supplierID</Ind>
244              <Var type="ID">sid</Var>
245          </slot>
246          <slot>
247              <Ind>productCategoryID</Ind>
248              <Var type="ID">pid</Var>
249          </slot>
250      </Atom>
251 </Implies>
252 <!-- Discount Policy 1-->
253 <Implies>
254      <!-- body -->
255      <Atom>
256              <Rel>hasCard</Rel>
257              <Var>client</Var>
258              <Ind>ProviderCard</Ind>
259      </Atom>
260      <!-- head -->
261      <Atom>
262              <Rel>getDiscount</Rel>
263              <Var>client</Var>
264              <Ind type="DiscountPercent">5</Ind>
265      </Atom>
266 </Implies>
267 <!--Discount Policy 2-->
268 <Implies>
269      <!-- body -->
270      <Atom>
271              <Rel>memberOf</Rel>
272              <Var type="Client">client</Var>
```

```
273              <Ind>PlatinumClub</Ind>
274          </Atom>
275          <!-- head -->
276          <Atom>
277              <Rel>getDiscount</Rel>
278              <Var type="Client">client</Var>
279              <Ind type="DiscountPercent">10</Ind>
280          </Atom>
281  </Implies>
282  <Implies>
283          <!-- Body -->
284          <Atom>
285              <Rel>hasCard</Rel>
286              <Var>client</Var>
287              <Var>card</Var>
288          </Atom>
289          <!-- Head -->
290          <Atom>
291              <Rel>getProviderCardHolder</Rel>
292              <Var>client</Var>
293              <Var>card</Var>
294          </Atom>
295  </Implies>
296  <!--Platinum Club Member SEarch Rule-->
297  <Implies>
298          <!-- Body -->
299          <Atom>
300              <Rel>memberOf</Rel>
301              <Var type="Client">client</Var>
302              <Var>club</Var>
303          </Atom>
304          <!-- Head -->
305          <Atom>
306              <Rel>getPlatinumMember</Rel>
307              <Var type="Client">client</Var>
308              <Var>club</Var>
309          </Atom>
310  </Implies>
311  <!-- Action History Rule -->
312  <Implies>
313          <!-- Body -->
314          <Atom>
315              <Rel>actionHistory</Rel>
316              <Var>payment_evt</Var>
317              <Var type="Payee">client</Var>
318              <Var type="Action">action</Var>
319              <Var type="Entity">resource</Var>
320                  <slot>
321                  <Ind>time</Ind>
322                  <Plex>
323                  <slot>
324                          <Ind>startTime</Ind>
325                          <Var type="Date">t1</Var>
326                  </slot>
327                  <slot>
```

```xml
                                        <Ind>endTime</Ind>
                                        <Var type="Date">t2</Var>
                            </slot>
                            </Plex>
                                            </slot>
            </Atom>
            <!-- Head -->
            <Atom>
                    <Rel>getActionHistory</Rel>
                    <Var>payment_evt</Var>
                    <Var type="Payee">client</Var>
                    <Var type="Action">action</Var>
                    <Var type="Entity">resource</Var>
                    <slot>
                    <Ind>time</Ind>
                    <Plex>
                    <slot>
                    <Ind>startTime</Ind>
                    <Var type="Date">t1</Var>
                    </slot>
                    <slot>
                    <Ind>endTime</Ind>
                    <Var type="Date">t2</Var>
                    </slot>
                    </Plex>
                    </slot>
            </Atom>
</Implies>
<!-- Big Spender Discount Rule -->
<Implies>
    <!-- Body -->
        <And>
                    <Atom>
                        <Rel>bigSpender</Rel>
                        <Var type="Payee">client</Var>
                        <Var type="Manufacturer">supplier</Var>
                    </Atom>
                    <Atom>
                        <Rel>actionHistory</Rel>
                        <Ind>payment_evt</Ind>
                        <Var type="Payee">client</Var>
                        <Var type="Action">action</Var>
                        <Var type="Entity">resource</Var>
                        <slot>
                            <Ind>time</Ind>
                            <Plex>
                                <slot>
                                    <Ind>startTime</Ind>
                                    <Var type="Date">t1</Var>
                                </slot>
                                <slot>
                                    <Ind>endTime</Ind>
                                    <Var type="Date">t2</Var>
                                </slot>
                            </Plex>
```

```
383              </slot>
384            </Atom>
385          </And>
386          <!-- Head -->
387          <Atom>
388            <Rel>getDiscount</Rel>
389            <Var type="Payee">client</Var>
390            <Var type="Manufacturer">supplier</Var>
391            <Ind type="DiscountPercent">10</Ind>
392          </Atom>
393        </Implies>
```

Appendix C: Policy KB

Listing 4: Partonomy of Business Processes

```
1  %Partonomy of Ordering Business Process
2
3  partOfProcess(order, issuePO).    % issuePO:Issuing PO
4  partOfProcess(order, responsePO). % responsePO: Responding PO
5  partOfProcess(order, requestPOChange).
6  partOfProcess(order, changePO).    % changePO: Changing PO
7  partOfProcess(order, cancelPO).    % cancelPO: Cancelling PO
8
9  %Partonomy of Despatching Business Process
10
11 partOfProcess(despatch, issueShipment).
12 partOfProcess(despatch, issueReceipt).
13
14 %Partonomy of Invoicing Business Process
15
16 partOfProcess(invoice, issueInvoice).
17 partOfProcess(invoice, issuePay).
18 partOfProcess(invoice, payBill).
19 partOfProcess(invoice, issueRemitBill).
20 partOfProcess(invoice, receivePay).
21
22 %Partonomy of Sourcing Business Process
23
24 partOfProcess(source, sendPriceList).
25 partOfProcess(source, requestQoute).    % reqQoute: requesting Qoute
26 partOfProcess(source, issueQoute).
27
28 %Partonomy Rule
29 getPartOfProcess(?process, ?subprocess) <— partOfProcess(?process, ?
      subprocess).
```

Listing 5: Procurement KB in RuleML

```
30 <Assert xmlns="http://www.ruleml.org/0.91/xsd" xmlns:xsi="http://www.w3
      .org/2001/XMLSchema-instance" xsi:schemaLocation="http://www.ruleml.
      org/0.91/xsd_http://www.ruleml.org/0.91/xsd/nafhornlog.xsd">
   <Rulebase mapClosure="universal">
32 <!— Partonomy of Ordering Business Process —>
   <Atom>
34       <Rel>partOfProcess</Rel>
         <Ind>order</Ind>
36       <Ind>issuePO</Ind>
   </Atom>
38 <Atom>
         <Rel>partOfProcess</Rel>
40       <Ind>order</Ind>
         <Ind>responsePO</Ind>
42 </Atom>
   <Atom>
44       <Rel>partOfProcess</Rel>
         <Ind>order</Ind>
46       <Ind>requestPOChange</Ind>
```

```
   </Atom>
48 <Atom>
           <Rel>partOfProcess</Rel>
50         <Ind>order</Ind>
           <Ind>changePO</Ind>
52 </Atom>
   <Atom>
54         <Rel>partOfProcess</Rel>
           <Ind>order</Ind>
56         <Ind>cancelPO</Ind>
   </Atom>
58 <Atom>
                           <Rel>bigSpender</Rel>
60                         <Ind type="Payee">client_131</Ind>
                           <Ind type="Manufacturer">s001222</Ind>
62              </Atom>
                <Atom>
64                         <Rel>bigSpender</Rel>
                           <Ind type="Payee">client_114</Ind>
66                         <Ind type="Manufacturer">s0033295</Ind>
                </Atom>
68              <Atom>
                           <Rel>bigSpender</Rel>
70                         <Ind type="Payee">client_111</Ind>
                           <Ind type="Manufacturer">s0033295</Ind>
72              </Atom>
                <Atom>
74                         <Rel>bigSpender</Rel>
                           <Ind type="Payee">client_43</Ind>
76                         <Ind type="Manufacturer">s0033295</Ind>
                </Atom>
78 <!-- Partonomy of Despatching Business Process -->
   <Atom>
80         <Rel>partOfProcess</Rel>
           <Ind>despatch</Ind>
82         <Ind>issueReceipt</Ind>
   </Atom>
84 <Atom>
           <Rel>partOfProcess</Rel>
86         <Ind>despatch</Ind>
           <Ind>iussueShipment</Ind>
88 </Atom>
   <!-- Partonomy of Invoicing Business Process -->
90 <Atom>
           <Rel>partOfProcess</Rel>
92         <Ind>invoice</Ind>
           <Ind>issueInvoice</Ind>
94 </Atom>
   <Atom>
96         <Rel>partOfProcess</Rel>
           <Ind>invoice</Ind>
98         <Ind>issuePay</Ind>
   </Atom>
100 <Atom>
           <Rel>partOfProcess</Rel>
```

```
102          <Ind>invoice</Ind>
             <Ind>payBill</Ind>
104  </Atom>
     <Atom>
106          <Rel>partOfProcess</Rel>
             <Ind>invoice</Ind>
108          <Ind>issueRemitBill</Ind>
     </Atom>
110  <Atom>
             <Rel>partOfProcess</Rel>
112          <Ind>invoice</Ind>
             <Ind>receivePay</Ind>
114  </Atom>
     <!--- Partonomy of Sourcing Business Process --->
116  <Atom>
             <Rel>partOfProcess</Rel>
118          <Ind>source</Ind>
             <Ind>sendPriceList</Ind>
120  </Atom>
     <Atom>
122          <Rel>partOfProcess</Rel>
             <Ind>source</Ind>
124          <Ind>requestQuote</Ind>
     </Atom>
126  <Atom>
             <Rel>partOfProcess</Rel>
128          <Ind>source</Ind>
             <Ind>issueQuote</Ind>
130  </Atom>

132  <!--- Product Category Fact--->
             <Atom>
134                  <Rel>productCategory</Rel>
                     <Ind type="ID">1</Ind>
136                  <Ind type="ProductAtt">raw material</Ind>
             </Atom>
138          <Atom>
                     <Rel>productCategory</Rel>
140                  <Ind type="ID">2</Ind>
                     <Ind type="ProductAtt">packaging</Ind>
142          </Atom>
             <Atom>
144                  <Rel>productCategory</Rel>
                     <Ind type="ID">3</Ind>
146                  <Ind type="ProductAtt">materials and services</Ind>
             </Atom>
148          <Atom>
                     <Rel>productCategory</Rel>
150                  <Ind type="ID">4</Ind>
                     <Ind type="ProductAtt">office supplies</Ind>
152          </Atom>
             <Atom>
154                  <Rel>productCategory</Rel>
                     <Ind type="ID">5</Ind>
156                  <Ind type="ProductAtt">marketing</Ind>
```

```
            </Atom>
158         <Atom>
                    <Rel>productCategory</Rel>
160                 <Ind type="ID">6</Ind>
                    <Ind type="ProductAtt">transportation</Ind>
162         </Atom>
            <Atom>
164                 <Rel>productCategory</Rel>
                    <Ind type="ID">7</Ind>
166                 <Ind type="ProductAtt">energy</Ind>
            </Atom>
168                 <!-- Maintenance, Repair and Operation -->
            <Atom>
170                 <Rel>productCategory</Rel>
                    <Ind type="ID">8</Ind>
172                 <Ind type="ProductAtt">MRO</Ind>
            </Atom>
174 <!-- Warranty Facts -->
        <Atom>
176             <Rel>warranty</Rel>
                <Ind type="ID">1</Ind>
178             <Ind type="Year">2</Ind>
        </Atom>
180     <Atom>
                <Rel>warranty</Rel>
182             <Ind type="ID">2</Ind>
                <Ind type="Year">2</Ind>
184     </Atom>
        <Atom>
186             <Rel>warranty</Rel>
                <Ind type="ID">3</Ind>
188             <Ind type="Year">2</Ind>
        </Atom>
190     <Atom>
                <Rel>warranty</Rel>
192             <Ind type="ID">4</Ind>
                <Ind type="Year">2</Ind>
194     </Atom>
        <Atom>
196             <Rel>warranty</Rel>
                <Ind type="ID">5</Ind>
198             <Ind type="Year">2</Ind>
        </Atom>
200     <Atom>
                <Rel>warranty</Rel>
202             <Ind type="ID">6</Ind>
                <Ind type="Year">2</Ind>
204     </Atom>
        <Atom>
206             <Rel>warranty</Rel>
                <Ind type="ID">7</Ind>
208             <Ind type="Year">2</Ind>
        </Atom>
210     <Atom>
                <Rel>warranty</Rel>
```

```
212         <Ind type="ID">8</Ind>
            <Ind type="Year">2</Ind>
214     </Atom>
        <Atom>
216         <Rel>product</Rel>
            <Ind type="ProductID">p002</Ind>
218         <Ind type="ProductName">Alu Foil</Ind>
            <Ind type="UnitPrice">50</Ind>
220         <Ind type="ProductQuantity">20000</Ind>
            <Ind type="Manufacturer">AluFoil Product Co.</Ind>
222         <Ind type="Description">large stocks of aluminium foil in
              various
              gauges, alloys and tempers, and are able to slit, sheet,
               press shapes and rewind.</Ind>
224         <slot>
                <Ind>supplierID</Ind>
226             <Ind type="ID">s-100143</Ind>
            </slot>
228         <slot>
                <Ind>productCategoryID</Ind>
230             <Ind type="ID">2</Ind>
            </slot>
232     </Atom>
        <Atom>
234         <Rel>product</Rel>
            <Ind type="ProductID">p003</Ind>
236         <Ind type="ProductName">Plastic Jars</Ind>
            <Ind type="UnitPrice">11</Ind>
238         <Ind type="ProductQuantity">540303</Ind>
            <Ind type="Manufacturer">LGPS</Ind>
240         <Ind type="Description">Just Plastic Jars</Ind>
            <slot>
242             <Ind>supplierID</Ind>
                <Ind type="ID">s-120331</Ind>
244         </slot>
            <slot>
246             <Ind>productCategoryID</Ind>
                <Ind type="ID">2</Ind>
248         </slot>
        </Atom>
250     <Atom>
            <Rel>product</Rel>
252         <Ind type="ProductID">p004</Ind>
            <Ind type="ProductName">Fiber-based Packaging</Ind>
254         <Ind type="UnitPrice">140</Ind>
            <Ind type="ProductQuantity">200000</Ind>
256         <Ind type="Manufacturer">LGPS</Ind>
            <Ind type="Description">Used to package all kinds of food</
              Ind>
258         <slot>
                <Ind>supplierID</Ind>
260             <Ind type="ID">s-120331</Ind>
            </slot>
262         <slot>
                <Ind>productCategoryID</Ind>
```

```
264                     <Ind type="ID">2</Ind>
                    </slot>
266         </Atom>
           <Atom>
268             <Rel>product</Rel>
                <Ind type="ProductID">p005</Ind>
270             <Ind type="ProductName">Tin</Ind>
                <Ind type="UnitPrice">12</Ind>
272             <Ind type="ProductQuantity">20000000</Ind>
                <Ind type="Manufacturer">LPGS</Ind>
274             <Ind type="Description">A soft pliable metal, but it is not
                    used
                as such because, below 13C</Ind>
276             <slot>
                    <Ind>supplierID</Ind>
278                     <Ind type="ID">s-103450</Ind>
                </slot>
280             <slot>
                    <Ind>productCategoryID</Ind>
282                     <Ind type="ID">2</Ind>
                </slot>
284         </Atom>
           <Atom>
286             <Rel>product</Rel>
                <Ind type="ProductID">os001</Ind>
288             <Ind type="ProductName">Pen</Ind>
                <Ind type="UnitPrice">3</Ind>
290             <Ind type="ProductQuantity">123456</Ind>
                <Ind type="Manufacturer">WholeSale Pen</Ind>
292              <Ind type="Description">Ballpoint pen, All colors,
                    Customize pens</Ind>
                <slot>
294                 <Ind>supplierID</Ind>
                    <Ind type="ID">s-180632</Ind>
296             </slot>
                <slot>
298                 <Ind>productCategoryID</Ind>
                    <Ind type="ID">3</Ind>
300             </slot>
           </Atom>
302        <Atom>
                <Rel>product</Rel>
304             <Ind type="ProductID">os002</Ind>
                <Ind type="ProductName">Book</Ind>
306             <Ind type="UnitPrice">3</Ind>
                <Ind type="ProductQuantity">20000</Ind>
308             <Ind type="Manufacturer">BookMakers Group</Ind>
                <Ind type="Description">Both Offset and digital books</Ind>
310             <slot>
                    <Ind>supplierID</Ind>
312                     <Ind type="ID">s-011112</Ind>
                </slot>
314             <slot>
                    <Ind>productCategoryID</Ind>
316                     <Ind type="ID">3</Ind>
```

```
                    </slot>
318              </Atom>
                 <Atom>
320                  <Rel>product</Rel>
                     <Ind type="ProductID">os003</Ind>
322                  <Ind type="ProductName">Paper</Ind>
                     <Ind type="UnitPrice">7</Ind>
324                  <Ind type="ProductQuantity">8000</Ind>
                     <Ind type="Manufacturer">James Cropper PLC</Ind>
326                  <slot>
                         <Ind>supplierID</Ind>
328                      <Ind type="ID">s-409210</Ind>
                     </slot>
330                  <Ind type="Description">A4, A3, All paper sizes</Ind>
                     <slot>
332                      <Ind>productCategoryID</Ind>
                         <Ind type="ID">3</Ind>
334                  </slot>
                 </Atom>
336              <Atom>
                     <Rel>product</Rel>
338                  <Ind type="ProductID">os004</Ind>
                     <Ind type="ProductName">Envelope</Ind>
340                  <Ind type="UnitPrice">1</Ind>
                     <Ind type="ProductQuantity">1500000</Ind>
342                  <Ind type="Manufacturer">Royal Mail</Ind>
                     <Ind type="Description">Specialized envelope styles and
                       sizes are
344              based on common commercial, catalog, and booklet styles.</
                   Ind>
                     <slot>
346                      <Ind>supplierID</Ind>
                         <Ind type="ID">s-678012</Ind>
348                  </slot>
                     <slot>
350                      <Ind>productCategoryID</Ind>
                         <Ind type="ID">3</Ind>
352                  </slot>
                 </Atom>
354              <Atom>
                     <Rel>product</Rel>
356                  <Ind type="ProductID">s005</Ind>
                     <Ind type="ProductName">Postage Stamps</Ind>
358                  <Ind type="UnitPrice">32</Ind>
                     <Ind type="ProductQuantity">3000000</Ind>
360                  <Ind type="Manufacturer">Royal Mail</Ind>
                     <Ind type="Description">First Class Stamps;One-day Stamps</
                       Ind>
362                  <slot>
                         <Ind>supplierID</Ind>
364                      <Ind type="ID">s-222910</Ind>
                     </slot>
366                  <slot>
                         <Ind>productCategoryID</Ind>
368                      <Ind type="ID">3</Ind>
```

```
                </slot>
370         </Atom>
            <Atom>
372             <Rel>product</Rel>
                <Ind type="ProductID">s006</Ind>
374             <Ind type="ProductName">Ink and Toner</Ind>
                <Ind type="UnitPrice">20</Ind>
376             <Ind type="ProductQuantity">1500</Ind>
                <Ind type="Manufacturer">Epson Acrauler</Ind>
378             <Ind type="Description">Epson ink, High Capacity Black,
                    High Capacity Red</Ind>
                <slot>
380                 <Ind>supplierID</Ind>
                    <Ind type="ID">s-120987</Ind>
382             </slot>
                <slot>
384                 <Ind>productCategoryID</Ind>
                    <Ind type="ID">3</Ind>
386             </slot>
            </Atom>
388         <Atom>
                <Rel>product</Rel>
390             <Ind type="ProductID">s007</Ind>
                <Ind type="ProductName">Box Files</Ind>
392             <Ind type="UnitPrice">4.19</Ind>
                <Ind type="ProductQuantity">1450</Ind>
394             <Ind type="Manufacturer">Viking</Ind>
                <Ind type="Description">Viking Plastic Box File Black.372 x
                    277 x78 mm</Ind>
396             <slot>
                    <Ind>supplierID</Ind>
398                 <Ind type="ID">s-133339</Ind>
                </slot>
400             <slot>
                    <Ind>productCategoryID</Ind>
402                 <Ind type="ID">3</Ind>
                </slot>
404         </Atom>

406         <Atom>
                <Rel>product</Rel>
408             <Ind type="ProductID">29113171-3</Ind>
                <Ind type="ProductName">Rotors</Ind>
410             <Ind type="UnitPrice">150</Ind>
                <Ind type="ProductQuantity">1500</Ind>
412             <Ind type="Manufacturer">Magura Venti</Ind>
                <Ind type="Description"> Our rotors are made of material
                    upgraded from the OE standard of SAE J431 Class G3000
414             (30,000 psi in tensile strength, 187-241 in Brinell
                    hardness).</Ind>
                <slot>
416                 <Ind>supplierID</Ind>
                    <Ind type="ID">s-22215010</Ind>
418             </slot>
                <slot>
```

```
420          <Ind>productCategoryID</Ind>
             <Ind  type="ID">8</Ind>
422        </slot>
        </Atom>
424     <Atom>
           <Rel>product</Rel>
426        <Ind  type="ProductID">29113170−6</Ind>
           <Ind  type="ProductName">Rotary  equipment</Ind>
428        <Ind  type="UnitPrice">10050</Ind>
           <Ind  type="ProductQuantity">1200</Ind>
430        <Ind  type="Manufacturer">Rotary  Equipment  Services  Ltd</Ind
             >
           <Ind type="Description">We supply , Install , Repair ,
             Maintain ,
432            Condition  Monitor ,  Upgrade  and  Refurbish  all  your
                 Rotating  Equipment
           </Ind>
434        <slot>
               <Ind>supplierID</Ind>
436            <Ind  type="ID">s−199202210</Ind>
           </slot>
438        <slot>
               <Ind>productCategoryID</Ind>
440            <Ind  type="ID">8</Ind>
           </slot>
442      </Atom>
         <Atom>
444        <Rel>product</Rel>
           <Ind  type="ProductID">29112410−4</Ind>
446        <Ind  type="ProductName">Turbine  instruments</Ind>
           <Ind  type="UnitPrice">1200</Ind>
448        <Ind  type="ProductQuantity">40000000</Ind>
           <Ind  type="Manufacturer">Electric_Motors</Ind><Ind type="
             Description">It  provides  precision  turbine  flowmeters  and
450            flow  measurement  products  for  Automotive ,  Aerospace ,
                 Test &
           Measurement ,  Metrology</Ind>
452        <slot>
               <Ind>supplierID</Ind>
454            <Ind  type="ID">s−199202210</Ind>
           </slot>
456        <slot>
               <Ind>productCategoryID</Ind>
458            <Ind  type="ID">8</Ind>
           </slot>
460      </Atom>
         <Atom>
462        <Rel>product</Rel>
           <Ind  type="ProductID">29112400−1</Ind>
464        <Ind  type="ProductName">Turbines  equipment</Ind>
           <Ind  type="UnitPrice">300</Ind>
466        <Ind  type="ProductQuantity">1890</Ind>
           <Ind  type="Manufacturer">ECPlaza</Ind>
468        <Ind  type="Description">Gas−turbine  and  compressor
             equipment  to  oil
```

61

```
              and gas</Ind>
470           <slot>
                  <Ind>supplierID</Ind>
472               <Ind type="ID">s-199202210</Ind>
              </slot>
474           <slot>
                  <Ind>productCategoryID</Ind>
476               <Ind type="ID">8</Ind>
              </slot>
478       </Atom>

480       <Atom>
                          <Rel>memberOf</Rel>
482                       <Ind type="Client">client_5</Ind>
                          <Ind>PlatinumClub</Ind>
484       </Atom>
          <Atom>
486                       <Rel>memberOf</Rel>
                          <Ind type="Client">client_15</Ind>
488                       <Ind>PlatinumClub</Ind>
          </Atom>
490       <Atom>
                          <Rel>memberOf</Rel>
492                       <Ind type="Client">client_50</Ind>
                          <Ind>PlatinumClub</Ind>
494       </Atom>
          <Atom>
496                       <Rel>memberOf</Rel>
                          <Ind type="Client">client_12</Ind>
498                       <Ind>PlatinumClub</Ind>
          </Atom>
500       <Atom>
                          <Rel>memberOf</Rel>
502                       <Ind type="Client">client_8</Ind>
                          <Ind>PlatinumClub</Ind>
504       </Atom>
          <Atom>
506                       <Rel>memberOf</Rel>
                          <Ind type="Client">client_7</Ind>
508                       <Ind>PlatinumClub</Ind>
          </Atom>
510       <Atom>
                          <Rel>memberOf</Rel>
512                       <Ind type="Client">client_6</Ind>
                          <Ind>PlatinumClub</Ind>
514       </Atom>
          <Atom>
516                       <Rel>memberOf</Rel>
                          <Ind type="Client">client_9</Ind>
518                       <Ind>PlatinumClub</Ind>
          </Atom>
520       <Atom>
                          <Rel>memberOf</Rel>
522                       <Ind type="Client">client_10</Ind>
                          <Ind>PlatinumClub</Ind>
```

```
524              </Atom>
              <Atom>
526                            <Rel>memberOf</Rel>
                             <Ind type="Client">client_11</Ind>
528                            <Ind>PlatinumClub</Ind>
              </Atom>
530   <Atom>
                             <Rel>hasCard</Rel>
532                          <Ind>client_1</Ind>
                             <Ind>ProviderCard</Ind>
534            </Atom>
              <Atom>
536                          <Rel>hasCard</Rel>
                             <Ind>client_20</Ind>
538                          <Ind>ProviderCard</Ind>
              </Atom>
540           <Atom>
                             <Rel>hasCard</Rel>
542                          <Ind>client_2</Ind>
                             <Ind>ProviderCard</Ind>
544           </Atom>
              <Atom>
546                          <Rel>hasCard</Rel>
                             <Ind>client_3</Ind>
548                          <Ind>ProviderCard</Ind>
              </Atom>
550           <Atom>
                             <Rel>hasCard</Rel>
552                          <Ind>client_4</Ind>
                             <Ind>ProviderCard</Ind>
554           </Atom>
   <Atom>
556           <Rel>supplier</Rel>
              <slot>
558                <Ind>companyInfo</Ind>
                   <Plex>
560                    <Ind type="ID">dk-3292-1120-12</Ind>
                       <Ind type="Company">Demsey Marketing Ltd</Ind>
562                    <Ind type="Description">Marketing and Stuff</Ind>
                       <Ind type="City">London</Ind>
564                    <Ind type="Country">UK</Ind>
                       <Ind type="TelePhone">+448920002213</Ind>
566                    <Ind type="URI">http://www.demsey.co.uk</Ind>
                       <Ind type="Email">aopemaet@demsey.com</Ind>
568                </Plex>
              </slot>
570           <slot>
                   <Ind>contactPerson</Ind>
572                <Plex>
                       <Ind type="ContactName">James Bolds</Ind>
574                    <Ind type="JobTitle">Marketing Manager</Ind>
                       <Ind type="TelePhone">+44012883922</Ind>
576                    <Ind type="Email">james.bolds@demsey.com</Ind>
                   </Plex>
578           </slot>
```

```
            <slot>
                <Ind>companyProfile</Ind>
                <Plex>
                    <slot>
                        <Ind>productCategory</Ind>
                        <Ind type="ID">5</Ind>
                    </slot>
                    <Ind type="LOB">Marketing and All</Ind>
                    <Ind type="TransportMode">Air ,Road</Ind>
                    <Ind type="Actor">Manufacturer</Ind>
                </Plex>
            </slot>
        </Atom>
    <Atom>
            <Rel>supplier</Rel>
            <slot>
                <Ind>companyInfo</Ind>
                <Plex>
                    <Ind type="ID">sd-3202-1212-13</Ind>
                    <Ind type="Company">Fansoft Ltd</Ind>
                    <Ind type="Description">Offer Office supplies</Ind>
                    <Ind type="City">London</Ind>
                    <Ind type="Country">UK</Ind>
                    <Ind type="TelePhone">020102990101</Ind>
                    <Ind type="URI">http://www.fansoft.co.uk</Ind>
                    <Ind type="Email">company@fansoft.com</Ind>
                </Plex>
            </slot>
            <slot>
                <Ind>contactPerson</Ind>
                <Plex>
                    <Ind type="ContactName">David Sampsons</Ind>
                    <Ind type="JobTitle">Manager</Ind>
                    <Ind type="TelePhone">+4413209333922</Ind>
                    <Ind type="Email">david.sampsons@fansoft.com</Ind>
                </Plex>
            </slot>
            <slot>
                <Ind>companyProfile</Ind>
                <Plex>
                    <slot>
                        <Ind>productCategory</Ind>
                        <Ind type="ID">4</Ind>
                    </slot>
                    <Ind type="LOB">Office Supplies</Ind>
                    <Ind type="TransportMode">Air</Ind>
                    <Ind type="Actor">Agent</Ind>
                </Plex>
            </slot>
        </Atom>
    <Atom>
            <Rel>supplier</Rel>
            <slot>
                <Ind>companyInfo</Ind>
                <Plex>
```

```
                              <Ind type="ID">s-199202210</Ind>
                              <Ind type="Company">GE</Ind>
                              <Ind type="Description">General Electronic Stuff</
                                 Ind>
                              <Ind type="City">London</Ind>
                              <Ind type="Country">UK</Ind>
                              <Ind type="TelePhone">+448920002213</Ind>
                              <Ind type="URI">http://www.demsey.co.uk</Ind>
                              <Ind type="Email">aopemaet@demsey.com</Ind>
                         </Plex>
                    </slot>
                    <slot>
                         <Ind>contactPerson</Ind>
                         <Plex>
                              <Ind type="ContactName">James Sweety</Ind>
                              <Ind type="JobTitle">Marketing Manager</Ind>
                              <Ind type="TelePhone">+44042883989</Ind>
                              <Ind type="Email">james.sweet@ge.com</Ind>
                         </Plex>
                    </slot>
                    <slot>
                         <Ind>companyProfile</Ind>
                         <Plex>
                              <slot>
                                   <Ind>productCategory</Ind>
                                   <Ind type="ID">8</Ind>
                              </slot>
                              <Ind type="LOB">Electrical Equipment</Ind>
                              <Ind type="TransportMode">Air</Ind>
                              <Ind type="Actor">Manufacturer</Ind>
                         </Plex>
                    </slot>
               </Atom>
     <Atom>
                    <Rel>supplier</Rel>
                    <slot>
                         <Ind>companyInfo</Ind>
                         <Plex>
                              <Ind type="ID">s-22215010</Ind>
                              <Ind type="Company">Rotor UK</Ind>
                              <Ind type="Description">When you require a motor,
                                 you can rely
                              on rotor </Ind>
                              <Ind type="City">London</Ind>
                              <Ind type="Country">UK</Ind>
                              <Ind type="TelePhone">+448920002213</Ind>
                              <Ind type="URI">http://www.rotor.co.uk</Ind>
                              <Ind type="Email">ask@rotor.com</Ind>
                         </Plex>
                    </slot>
                    <slot>
                         <Ind>contactPerson</Ind>
                         <Plex>
                              <Ind type="ContactName">James Bolds</Ind>
                              <Ind type="JobTitle">Marketing Manager</Ind>
```

```
688                        <Ind type="TelePhone">+44012883922</Ind>
                           <Ind type="Email">james.bolds@rotor.com</Ind>
                        </Plex>
690                    </slot>
                    <slot>
692                        <Ind>companyProfile</Ind>
                        <Plex>
694                            <slot>
                                <Ind>productCategory</Ind>
696                                <Ind type="ID">8</Ind>
                            </slot>
                            <Ind type="LOB">Rotor</Ind>
698                            <Ind type="TransportMode">Air</Ind>
                            <Ind type="Actor">Manufacturer</Ind>
700                        </Plex>
                    </slot>
702                </slot>
            </Atom>
704  <Atom>
            <Rel>actionHistory</Rel>
706         <Ind>payment_evt</Ind>
            <Ind type="Payee">client_111</Ind>
708         <Ind type="Action">payment_action</Ind>
            <Ind type="Entity">PVA</Ind>
710         <slot>
                <Ind>time</Ind>
712             <Plex>
                    <slot>
714                     <Ind>startTime</Ind>
                        <Ind type="Date">13/04/2010:1200AM</Ind
                        >
716                     </slot>
                    <slot>
718                     <Ind>endTime</Ind>
                        <Ind type="Date">13/04/2010:1300PM</Ind
                        >
720                     </slot>
                </Plex>
722         </slot>
    </Atom>
724         <Atom>
                <Rel>actionHistory</Rel>
726             <Ind>payment_evt</Ind>
                <Ind type="Payee">client_43</Ind>
728             <Ind type="Action">payment_action</Ind>
                <Ind type="Entity">Paper</Ind>
730             <slot>
                    <Ind>time</Ind>
732                 <Plex>
                        <slot>
734                         <Ind>startTime</Ind>
                            <Ind type="Date">10/02/2010
                            :0800AM</Ind>
736                         </slot>
                        <slot>
738                         <Ind>endTime</Ind>
```

66

```
                                                        <Ind type="Date">10/02/2010
                                                            :0900AM</Ind>
                                            </slot>
                                    </Plex>
                            </slot>
                    </Atom>
                    <Atom>
                            <Rel>actionHistory</Rel>
                            <Ind>payment_evt</Ind>
                            <Ind type="Payee">client_114</Ind>
                            <Ind type="Action">payment_action</Ind>
                            <Ind type="Entity">Rotor</Ind>
                            <slot>
                                    <Ind>time</Ind>
                                    <Plex>
                                            <slot>
                                                    <Ind>startTime</Ind>
                                                    <Ind type="Date">01/01/2009
                                                        :1430PM</Ind>
                                            </slot>
                                            <slot>
                                                    <Ind>endTime</Ind>
                                                    <Ind type="Date">01/01/2009
                                                        :1640PM</Ind>
                                            </slot>
                                    </Plex>
                            </slot>
                    </Atom>
                    <Atom>
                            <Rel>actionHistory</Rel>
                            <Ind>payment_evt</Ind>
                            <Ind type="Payee">client_131</Ind>
                            <Ind type="Action">payment_action</Ind>
                            <Ind type="Entity">Resin</Ind>
                            <slot>
                                    <Ind>time</Ind>
                                    <Plex>
                                            <slot>
                                                    <Ind>startTime</Ind>
                                                    <Ind type="Date">28/08/2010
                                                        :1745PM</Ind>
                                            </slot>
                                            <slot>
                                                    <Ind>endTime</Ind>
                                                    <Ind type="Date">28/08/2010
                                                        :1912PM</Ind>
                                            </slot>
                                    </Plex>
                            </slot>
                    </Atom>

</Rulebase>
</Assert>
```

Appendix D: RDFS Type Definitions

Listing 6: Access Control and E-Procurement Domain Ontology

```
1  <rdf:RDF xmlns:rdf="http://www.w3.org/1999/02/22-rdf-syntax-ns#"
           xmlns:rdfs="http://www.w3.org/2000/01/rdf-schema#" xml:base="
           http://www.owl-ontologies.com/">
3          <rdfs:Class rdf:ID="Active">
                   <rdfs:subClassOf>
5                          <rdfs:Class rdf:ID="ActionStatus" />
                   </rdfs:subClassOf>
7          </rdfs:Class>
           <rdfs:Class rdf:ID="Year">
9                  <rdfs:subClassOf>
                           <rdfs:Class rdf:ID="Attribute" />
11                 </rdfs:subClassOf>
           </rdfs:Class>
13         <rdfs:Class rdf:ID="TransportMode">
                   <rdfs:subClassOf>
15                         <rdfs:Class rdf:ID="Attribute" />
                   </rdfs:subClassOf>
17         </rdfs:Class>
           <rdfs:Class rdf:ID="LineID">
19                 <rdfs:subClassOf rdf:resource="#Attribute" />
           </rdfs:Class>
21         <rdfs:Class rdf:ID="Client">
                   <rdfs:subClassOf>
23                         <rdfs:Class rdf:ID="Actor" />
                   </rdfs:subClassOf>
25         </rdfs:Class>
           <rdfs:Class rdf:ID="CallPropose">
27                 <rdfs:subClassOf>
                           <rdfs:Class rdf:ID="Message" />
29                 </rdfs:subClassOf>
           </rdfs:Class>
31         <rdfs:Class rdf:ID="DespatchAction">
                   <rdfs:subClassOf>
33                         <rdfs:Class rdf:ID="Action" />
                   </rdfs:subClassOf>
35         </rdfs:Class>
           <rdfs:Class rdf:ID="Consignee">
37                 <rdfs:subClassOf rdf:resource="#Actor" />
           </rdfs:Class>
39         <rdfs:Class rdf:ID="AddressType">
                   <rdfs:subClassOf rdf:resource="#Attribute" />
41         </rdfs:Class>
           <rdfs:Class rdf:ID="Broker">
43                 <rdfs:subClassOf rdf:resource="#Actor" />
           </rdfs:Class>
45         <rdfs:Class rdf:ID="Suspended">
                   <rdfs:subClassOf rdf:resource="#ActionStatus" />
47         </rdfs:Class>
           <rdfs:Class rdf:ID="Date">
49                 <rdfs:subClassOf rdf:resource="#Attribute" />
           </rdfs:Class>
51         <rdfs:Class rdf:ID="Amount">
```

```xml
            <rdfs:subClassOf rdf:resource="#Attribute" />
        </rdfs:Class>
        <rdfs:Class rdf:ID="Policy" />
        <rdfs:Class rdf:ID="StreetName">
            <rdfs:subClassOf rdf:resource="#Attribute" />
        </rdfs:Class>
        <rdfs:Class rdf:ID="POAccept">
            <rdfs:subClassOf>
                    <rdfs:Class rdf:ID="BOD" />
            </rdfs:subClassOf>
        </rdfs:Class>
        <rdfs:Class rdf:ID="TotalPrice">
            <rdfs:subClassOf rdf:resource="#Attribute" />
        </rdfs:Class>
        <rdfs:Class rdf:ID="Cancel">
            <rdfs:subClassOf rdf:resource="#Message" />
        </rdfs:Class>
        <rdfs:Class rdf:ID="OrganName">
            <rdfs:subClassOf rdf:resource="#Attribute" />
        </rdfs:Class>
        <rdfs:Class rdf:ID="LineItem">
            <rdfs:subClassOf rdf:resource="#Attribute" />
        </rdfs:Class>
        <rdfs:Class rdf:ID="Payee">
            <rdfs:subClassOf rdf:resource="#Actor" />
        </rdfs:Class>
        <rdfs:Class rdf:ID="PartyName">
            <rdfs:subClassOf rdf:resource="#Attribute" />
        </rdfs:Class>
        <rdfs:Class rdf:ID="Manufacturer">
            <rdfs:subClassOf rdf:resource="#Actor" />
        </rdfs:Class>
        <rdfs:Class rdf:ID="Confirm">
            <rdfs:subClassOf rdf:resource="#Message" />
        </rdfs:Class>
        <rdfs:Class rdf:ID="AccountNumber">
            <rdfs:subClassOf rdf:resource="#Attribute" />
        </rdfs:Class>
        <rdfs:Class rdf:ID="FaxNumber">
            <rdfs:subClassOf rdf:resource="#Attribute" />
        </rdfs:Class>
        <rdfs:Class rdf:ID="TaxAmt">
            <rdfs:subClassOf rdf:resource="#Attribute" />
        </rdfs:Class>
        <rdfs:Class rdf:ID="InActive">
            <rdfs:subClassOf rdf:resource="#ActionStatus" />
        </rdfs:Class>
        <rdfs:Class rdf:ID="CCDate">
            <rdfs:subClassOf rdf:resource="#Date" />
        </rdfs:Class>
        <rdfs:Class rdf:ID="UnitPrice">
            <rdfs:subClassOf rdf:resource="#Attribute" />
        </rdfs:Class>
        <rdfs:Class rdf:ID="Inform">
            <rdfs:subClassOf rdf:resource="#Message" />
```

```
107    </rdfs:Class>
       <rdfs:Class rdf:ID="OrderAction">
109        <rdfs:subClassOf rdf:resource="#Action" />
       </rdfs:Class>
111    <rdfs:Class rdf:ID="TaxDesc">
           <rdfs:subClassOf rdf:resource="#Attribute" />
113    </rdfs:Class>
       <rdfs:Class rdf:ID="Region">
115        <rdfs:subClassOf rdf:resource="#Attribute" />
       </rdfs:Class>
117    <rdfs:Class rdf:ID="Organization">
           <rdfs:subClassOf rdf:resource="#Actor" />
119    </rdfs:Class>
       <rdfs:Class rdf:ID="EffectiveDate">
121        <rdfs:subClassOf rdf:resource="#Date" />
       </rdfs:Class>
123    <rdfs:Class rdf:ID="ReqQuote">
           <rdfs:subClassOf>
125            <rdfs:Class rdf:about="#BOD" />
           </rdfs:subClassOf>
127    </rdfs:Class>
       <rdfs:Class rdf:ID="Request">
129        <rdfs:subClassOf rdf:resource="#Message" />
       </rdfs:Class>
131    <rdfs:Class rdf:ID="PaymentAction">
           <rdfs:subClassOf rdf:resource="#Action" />
133    </rdfs:Class>
       <rdfs:Class rdf:ID="PostalCode">
135        <rdfs:subClassOf rdf:resource="#Attribute" />
       </rdfs:Class>
137    <rdfs:Class rdf:ID="DeliveryNote">
           <rdfs:subClassOf>
139            <rdfs:Class rdf:about="#BOD" />
           </rdfs:subClassOf>
141    </rdfs:Class>
       <rdfs:Class rdf:ID="TaxAmount">
143        <rdfs:subClassOf rdf:resource="#Attribute" />
       </rdfs:Class>
145    <rdfs:Class rdf:ID="ProductCode">
           <rdfs:subClassOf rdf:resource="#Attribute" />
147    </rdfs:Class>
       <rdfs:Class rdf:ID="Currency">
149        <rdfs:subClassOf rdf:resource="#Attribute" />
       </rdfs:Class>
151    <rdfs:Class rdf:ID="ProductQuantity">
           <rdfs:subClassOf rdf:resource="#Attribute" />
153    </rdfs:Class>
       <rdfs:Class rdf:ID="Place" />
155    <rdfs:Class rdf:ID="ID">
           <rdfs:subClassOf rdf:resource="#Attribute" />
157    </rdfs:Class>
       <rdfs:Class rdf:ID="Agree">
159        <rdfs:subClassOf rdf:resource="#Message" />
       </rdfs:Class>
161    <rdfs:Class rdf:ID="Time">
```

```
                        <rdfs:subClassOf rdf:resource="#Attribute" />
163         </rdfs:Class>
        <rdfs:Class rdf:ID="Quotation">
165                 <rdfs:subClassOf>
                            <rdfs:Class rdf:about="#BOD" />
167                 </rdfs:subClassOf>
        </rdfs:Class>
169     <rdfs:Class rdf:ID="Rate">
                        <rdfs:subClassOf rdf:resource="#Attribute" />
171     </rdfs:Class>
        <rdfs:Class rdf:ID="Description">
173                 <rdfs:subClassOf rdf:resource="#Attribute" />
        </rdfs:Class>
175     <rdfs:Class rdf:ID="Payer">
                        <rdfs:subClassOf rdf:resource="#Actor" />
177     </rdfs:Class>
        <rdfs:Class rdf:ID="CompletionDate">
179                 <rdfs:subClassOf rdf:resource="#Date" />
        </rdfs:Class>
181     <rdfs:Class rdf:ID="Invoice">
                        <rdfs:subClassOf>
183                         <rdfs:Class rdf:about="#BOD" />
                        </rdfs:subClassOf>
185     </rdfs:Class>
        <rdfs:Class rdf:ID="ProductAtt">
187                 <rdfs:subClassOf rdf:resource="#Attribute" />
        </rdfs:Class>
189     <rdfs:Class rdf:ID="PersonSurname">
                        <rdfs:subClassOf rdf:resource="#Attribute" />
191     </rdfs:Class>
        <rdfs:Class rdf:ID="InvoiceAction">
193                 <rdfs:subClassOf rdf:resource="#Action" />
        </rdfs:Class>
195     <rdfs:Class rdf:ID="Entity" />
        <rdfs:Class rdf:ID="MeasureUnit">
197                 <rdfs:subClassOf rdf:resource="#Attribute" />
        </rdfs:Class>
199     <rdfs:Class rdf:ID="FreightForwarder">
                        <rdfs:subClassOf rdf:resource="#Actor" />
201     </rdfs:Class>
        <rdfs:Class rdf:ID="DeliveryDate">
203                 <rdfs:subClassOf rdf:resource="#Date" />
        </rdfs:Class>
205     <rdfs:Class rdf:ID="Seller">
                        <rdfs:subClassOf rdf:resource="#Actor" />
207     </rdfs:Class>
        <rdfs:Class rdf:ID="Financer">
209                 <rdfs:subClassOf rdf:resource="#Actor" />
        </rdfs:Class>
211     <rdfs:Class rdf:ID="Propose">
                        <rdfs:subClassOf rdf:resource="#Message" />
213     </rdfs:Class>
        <rdfs:Class rdf:ID="POCancel">
215                 <rdfs:subClassOf>
                            <rdfs:Class rdf:about="#BOD" />
```

```
217            </rdfs:subClassOf>
          </rdfs:Class>
219       <rdfs:Class rdf:ID="Country">
              <rdfs:subClassOf rdf:resource="#Attribute" />
221       </rdfs:Class>
          <rdfs:Class rdf:ID="RequestAction">
223           <rdfs:subClassOf rdf:resource="#Action" />
          </rdfs:Class>
225       <rdfs:Class rdf:ID="DocumentDate">
              <rdfs:subClassOf rdf:resource="#Date" />
227       </rdfs:Class>
          <rdfs:Class rdf:ID="Importer">
229           <rdfs:subClassOf rdf:resource="#Actor" />
          </rdfs:Class>
231       <rdfs:Class rdf:ID="Text">
              <rdfs:subClassOf rdf:resource="#Attribute" />
233       </rdfs:Class>
          <rdfs:Class rdf:ID="IssueAction">
235           <rdfs:subClassOf rdf:resource="#Action" />
          </rdfs:Class>
237       <rdfs:Class rdf:ID="AccountType">
              <rdfs:subClassOf rdf:resource="#Attribute" />
239       </rdfs:Class>
          <rdfs:Class rdf:ID="PostalAddress">
241           <rdfs:subClassOf rdf:resource="#Attribute" />
          </rdfs:Class>
243       <rdfs:Class rdf:ID="PurchaseOrder">
          <rdfs:subClassOf>
245                   <rdfs:Class rdf:about="#BOD" />
          </rdfs:subClassOf>
247       </rdfs:Class>
          <rdfs:Class rdf:ID="LineStatus">
249           <rdfs:subClassOf rdf:resource="#Attribute" />
          </rdfs:Class>
251       <rdfs:Class rdf:about="#BOD">
              <rdfs:subClassOf rdf:resource="#Entity" />
253       </rdfs:Class>
          <rdfs:Class rdf:ID="Person">
255           <rdfs:subClassOf rdf:resource="#Actor" />
          </rdfs:Class>
257       <rdfs:Class rdf:ID="PriceList">
              <rdfs:subClassOf rdf:resource="#BOD" />
259       </rdfs:Class>
          <rdfs:Class rdf:ID="TaxRate">
261           <rdfs:subClassOf rdf:resource="#Attribute" />
          </rdfs:Class>
263       <rdfs:Class rdf:ID="PersonName">
              <rdfs:subClassOf rdf:resource="#Attribute" />
265       </rdfs:Class>
          <rdfs:Class rdf:ID="ResponseAction">
267           <rdfs:subClassOf rdf:resource="#Action" />
          </rdfs:Class>
269       <rdfs:Class rdf:ID="ContactName">
              <rdfs:subClassOf rdf:resource="#Attribute" />
271       </rdfs:Class>
```

```
273    <rdfs:Class rdf:ID="EmailAddress">
           <rdfs:subClassOf rdf:resource="#Attribute" />
       </rdfs:Class>
275    <rdfs:Class rdf:ID="POReject">
           <rdfs:subClassOf rdf:resource="#BOD" />
277    </rdfs:Class>
       <rdfs:Class rdf:ID="Exporter">
279        <rdfs:subClassOf rdf:resource="#Actor" />
       </rdfs:Class>
281    <rdfs:Class rdf:ID="PartyID">
           <rdfs:subClassOf rdf:resource="#Attribute" />
283    </rdfs:Class>
       <rdfs:Class rdf:ID="ShipConfirm">
285        <rdfs:subClassOf rdf:resource="#BOD" />
       </rdfs:Class>
287    <rdfs:Class rdf:ID="SaleOrder">
           <rdfs:subClassOf rdf:resource="#BOD" />
289    </rdfs:Class>
       <rdfs:Class rdf:ID="PurchaseDate">
291        <rdfs:subClassOf rdf:resource="#Date" />
       </rdfs:Class>
293    <rdfs:Class rdf:ID="ExRDate">
           <rdfs:subClassOf rdf:resource="#Date" />
295    </rdfs:Class>
       <rdfs:Class rdf:ID="DiscountPercent">
297        <rdfs:subClassOf rdf:resource="#Attribute" />
       </rdfs:Class>
299    <rdfs:Class rdf:ID="PaymentMethod">
           <rdfs:subClassOf rdf:resource="#Attribute" />
301    </rdfs:Class>
       <rdfs:Class rdf:ID="Quantity">
303        <rdfs:subClassOf rdf:resource="#Attribute" />
       </rdfs:Class>
305    <rdfs:Class rdf:ID="ProductName">
           <rdfs:subClassOf rdf:resource="#Attribute" />
307    </rdfs:Class>
       <rdfs:Class rdf:ID="Quote">
309        <rdfs:subClassOf rdf:resource="#BOD" />
       </rdfs:Class>
311    <rdfs:Class rdf:ID="Language">
           <rdfs:subClassOf rdf:resource="#Attribute" />
313    </rdfs:Class>
       <rdfs:Class rdf:ID="CancelAction">
315        <rdfs:subClassOf rdf:resource="#Action" />
       </rdfs:Class>
317    <rdfs:Class rdf:ID="AccountName">
           <rdfs:subClassOf rdf:resource="#Attribute" />
319    </rdfs:Class>
       <rdfs:Class rdf:ID="ProductID">
321        <rdfs:subClassOf rdf:resource="#Attribute" />
       </rdfs:Class>
323    <rdfs:Class rdf:ID="Email">
           <rdfs:subClassOf rdf:resource="#Attribute" />
325    </rdfs:Class>
       <rdfs:Class rdf:ID="URI">
```

```
327          <rdfs:subClassOf rdf:resource="#Attribute" />
        </rdfs:Class>
329     <rdfs:Class rdf:ID="TelePhone">
             <rdfs:subClassOf rdf:resource="#Attribute" />
331     </rdfs:Class>
        <rdfs:Class rdf:ID="City">
333          <rdfs:subClassOf rdf:resource="#Attribute" />
        </rdfs:Class>
335     <rdfs:Class rdf:ID="JobTitle">
             <rdfs:subClassOf rdf:resource="#Attribute" />
337     </rdfs:Class>
        <rdfs:Class rdf:ID="LOB">
339          <rdfs:subClassOf rdf:resource="#Attribute" />
        </rdfs:Class>
341     <rdfs:Class rdf:ID="Company">
             <rdfs:subClassOf rdf:resource="#Attribute" />
343     </rdfs:Class>
        <rdfs:Class rdf:ID="ProductCategory">
345          <rdfs:subClassOf rdf:resource="#Attribute" />
        </rdfs:Class>
347     <rdfs:Class rdf:ID="OrderChange">
             <rdfs:subClassOf rdf:resource="#BOD" />
349     </rdfs:Class>
        <rdfs:Class rdf:ID="ActionHistory" />
351     <rdfs:Class rdf:ID="Telephone">
             <rdfs:subClassOf rdf:resource="#Attribute" />
353     </rdfs:Class>
        <rdfs:Class rdf:ID="POUpdate">
355          <rdfs:subClassOf rdf:resource="#BOD" />
        </rdfs:Class>
357 </rdf:RDF>
```

www.ingramcontent.com/pod-product-compliance
Lightning Source LLC
Chambersburg PA
CBHW041430050326
40690CB00002B/493